OUT HERE

Recent books by John Houghton include:

OUT HERE

a different way of being

JOHN HOUGHTON

NEXGEN

ISBN 1 84291 174 0

Published by
KINGSWAY COMMUNICATIONS LTD
Lottbridge Drove, Eastbourne BN23 6NT, England.
Email: books@kingsway.co.uk

Book design and production for the publishers by
Bookprint Creative Services, P.O. Box 827, BN21 3YJ, England.
Printed in Great Britain.

For the clan –
David and Maureen, Keith and Val, Geoff and Chris, in
appreciation of long years of love and friendship.

Contents

Acknowledgements

I have written this book to challenge and provoke God's people to seize the fresh opportunities all around them. In recent years I have been privileged to work with a number of teams and individuals who have helped shape my thinking. None of them are to blame for the outcome and they are too many to mention all by name but I wish to acknowledge the following who have shared the recent journey variously as pals, pioneers and practitioners: Cliff Allen, Andy Au, Alan Baker, Colin Blackman, Ian Chisnall, Sas Conradie, David and Maureen Craig, Tony Cross, Tony Denyer, Geoff and Chris Gobbett, David Hall, Nic Harding, Nigel and Ellen Hewitt, Bernie and Maureen Howe, Keith and Val Ives, Peter Johnson, Phil Keene, Dave King, Robert Mountford, Kevin Popely, Danny Pritchard, Martyn Relf, Dave Roberts, Martin Robinson, Alex Ross, Chris Seaton, Dwight Smith, Bob Street, John Swindell, Rob Watson, Paul Weaver, Bob and Kate Webb, Andy Whisker, Steve and Yvonne Wood.

To these may be added:

The Catalyst Ministries team that initiated mission strategy for East Sussex.

The Together in Mission team that is pioneering the future as a servant ministry to the denominations and regions of the land.

The Building Together South team that has captured the deep dynamic of the Spirit for unity, mission and transformation.

The Ashburnham Bible Week team that proved we could joint venture for a region without building an empire.

The Living Stones team, where the rubber hits the road.

Ordinary Christians

*I will give you as a light to the nations, that you may bring
my salvation to the end of the earth.* (Isaiah 49:6 RSV)

This book is about the way we ordinary Christians can make
a real difference to our world. Infinite possibilities in Christ
can be realised in the mundane and the routine of everyday
life. God can make our lives count without the need for glam-
orous ministry trips to exotic locations, or some special call
to the weird and wonderful. Ministry is about to take on a
new meaning; the glory of God is going to touch the common
place of our lives – and there are enough of us to change the
world!

What kind of people are we? Just ordinary men and women,
teenagers, young adults, perhaps not so young, who wake up
to Monday mornings of sluggish computers and ratty colleagues, kids who don't want to go to school, projects that
should have been in last Friday, and the dire prospect of
another church meeting to discuss the colour of paint. This is
our world, where we struggle to do our best but aren't always

sure what our best should be, except that it has something to do with being good witnesses to those around us.

For most of us it's easier said than done. Even when we've got our act together and our hearts are bopping to the latest praise song, we mostly find ourselves in an embarrassing minority and set in a culture where discussing religion is akin to mentioning a delicate personal problem. So we keep quiet and reserve our faith for safe environments, attending church and engaging our leisure time in programmes and activities that for all our zeal touch only the tiniest minorities in our communities. Hardly world changing!

Yet we truly believe that the gospel of our Lord Jesus Christ is the most wonderful news in the world. We know it has the power to transform lives and to transform whole societies. Haven't we read the books and heard the stories of what God is doing in different parts of the globe, and hoped that it might happen here too? Surely the message of Christ is supremely relevant to every sphere of human conduct: to everyday work, to education, to entertainment, the arts and media, to politics and health care, to family life and personal relationships, to science and technology, to the inner needs of every human being, to the search for a personal relationship with God? Our message is the truth that dispels lies, the light that overcomes darkness, that gives comfort for the dying and hope for the living. In Charles Wesley's great words, the name of Jesus speaks power into strengthless souls and life into the dead; it scatters all their guilty fear and turns their hell to heaven.

Why then this credibility gap between the reality of our daily routines and our beliefs and hopes and dreams?

The world should be welcoming such good news with open arms, and God's people should be proclaiming it with a passion that engages every single one of us in every aspect of our lives. Why then this credibility gap between the reality of our daily routines and the reality of our beliefs and hopes and dreams? Why the decline of the gospel in our land when it appears to flourish everywhere else? Something is wrong, and something needs to change.

We need an honest and radical rethink about how we conduct our daily lives. It isn't just a solo affair either; we are part of God's people together and we can only succeed if our churches and leaders are committed to the same path. So we need to reconsider the purpose of church, the role of its leaders and its relevance to our twenty-first-century society. What are we all here for? What changes should we make if we are to bring about the vision of a transformed society? How do we get connected in the first place? What is our part in all this?

If a definition of insanity is to repeat the same actions and expect a different result, then we are surely insane to carry on as we are. The men of Issachar 'understood the times and knew what Israel should do' (1 Chronicles 12:32). We must heed the voice of the prophets who understand what the Spirit is saying to the churches. Already many are; churches are beginning to change, ordinary people are being empowered for extraordinary possibilities.

Standing on the brink of change can be both exhilarating and terrifying. It simultaneously invites faith and induces fear. This book is an invitation to step over the threshold so that our faith becomes actual and our fear dissolves away in the discovery that God can do 'immeasurably more than all we ask or imagine, according to his power that is at work within us'. It is time to change and the journey starts here.

John Houghton

1

God's Missionary Society

A friend of ours said recently, 'John, what are you going to do? I mean, I'm now forty-two and it has taken me this long to find out what the Christian faith is all about. Nobody has ever told me before. Sure, I rejected Christianity as I saw it, but it's only recently that I discovered that what I rejected wasn't the real thing, anyway! How are you going to get the truth over to all the millions of people like me?'

How indeed? It's a fair challenge and one that nobody who bears the name of Christ can ignore or rationalise away.

Like me, you may be plain ordinary, with just a few highlights to brighten your story of subdued normality. The bulk of my life, and probably most people's, has been occupied with going to school, playing sport and developing hobbies, chilling out with friends, getting married, going to work, raising children, looking after the house, paying the bills and wanting a decent night's sleep. Yet, like me, in that ordinariness you are possessed by God's most extraordinary grace.

Just take a few moments to think about all that you have in Jesus:

- You have discovered the secret of life and have a wonderful destiny to fulfil.
- Your sins are forgiven and you have peace with God – a new heart and a fresh start.
- You are a child of God, chosen and adopted into his family.
- You are risen with Christ – eternal life starts right now!
- You are energised by the Holy Spirit – empowered for living!
- Jesus loves you and you will never be lonely again.
- You are an honoured part of Christ's body.
- You have a splendid future and Jesus will return for you.

Mentally remove all these blessings and their effects from your life story. Now you know how your neighbour feels.

Most of us know, sometimes enthusiastically, sometimes guiltily, that we are called to share our faith with others. Jesus left us with his commission to 'go and make disciples of all nations' (Matthew 28:18). Paul tells us that we are new creation people, reconciled to God and given the ministry of reconciliation. 'We are therefore Christ's ambassadors, as though God were making his appeal through us' (2 Corinthians 5:20). We have a vital part to play in God's great purpose in Christ 'to reconcile to himself all things, whether things on earth or things in heaven, by making peace through his blood shed on the cross' (Colossians 1:20). It is a call to join God's own missionary society.

Like me, you are probably tired of the manic evangelical tract urging us to reach the lost. I've had my fill of the Jesus product packaged for network selling and I don't want any more. Instead, I want to take you back to the drawing board – back to God's original plan for his people which transcends all our guilt-driven quick fixes and glitzy programmes for saving the world.

The mission of God, known among the experts as the *missio Dei*, goes far beyond what we popularly understand as evangelism and social action. Springing timelessly from his eternal and undying love, it touches every aspect of our existence and gives our ordinary lives a cosmic significance that is simply mind-blowing.

From the distant echoes of Eden to the heralding of the Holy City, one clear message rings out: God loves those made in his image and he wants fellowship with them. To know God is the point of all existence; the location in time and space of each one of us is 'so that men would seek him and perhaps reach out for him and find him, though he is not far from each one of us' (Acts 17:26–27). For Eden's catastrophe could not deter God from his purpose; Christ's sacrifice has transformed sin's tragedy into a comedy of grace. The day will come when he can say, 'Now the dwelling of God is with men, and he will live with them. They will be his people, and God himself will be with them and be their God' (Revelation 21:3).

Christ's sacrifice has transformed sin's tragedy into a comedy of grace.

The chief member of God's missionary society is Jesus, the Servant of the Lord, and this is his own mission manifesto: 'The Spirit of the Lord is on me, because he has anointed me to preach good news to the poor. He has sent me to proclaim freedom for the prisoners and recovery of sight for the blind, to release the oppressed, to proclaim the year of the Lord's favour' (Luke 4:18–19). All those in Christ share the same redemptive calling, for the body surely must serve the heart and will of the head.

The single purpose of the church

If mission is at the heart of God's will for his people, it follows
that the only way to glorify God is to make it the heart of our
churches. This is not simply the job of those who are so-called
'full time' or otherwise ordained. It is the permanent priestly
calling of all God's people all of the time and in every place.
Every one of us has a part to play in this ministry according
to the unique refraction of God's grace through each of our
differing personalities.

It goes without saying that we must take the message to
every nation and every people group on earth. That is our traditional understanding of missionary work. However, the
mission of God calls us to engage in all the spheres of the
world, as well as every geographic location. We are to be salt
and light in business and commerce, in education, in health
care, in the arts, in media, in science and technology, in social
welfare, in politics and government, in entertainment – whatever. Our task is to inform all these spheres with the wisdom
of Scripture and the blessings of the gospel in such a manner
as to bring about social transformation and cultural renewal.

This ministry of reconciliation requires that we engage with
the world, its agendas and its needs, identifying with its joys
and its pains alike. Paul describes Jesus as the one 'who fills
everything in every way' (Ephesians 1:23), and the writer to
the Hebrews says the Son is 'sustaining all things by his powerful word' (Hebrews 1:3). These are powerful statements
about the Lordship of Christ and of his incarnate presence in
all creation. Although the redemptive work of Calvary is in
one sense complete, in another sense it is ongoing. Creation
has yet to be liberated from its bondage to decay; the recon-

ciliation of all things still lies in the future. It is the omega point of history, the culmination of the mission of God. Meanwhile, Christ the Lord continues his Servant ministry, inhabiting the molecules of joy and sorrow, filling every particle with his transcendent presence, working towards that glorious goal.

There can be no secular world separate from a sacred world. Christ's fullness sanctifies concrete parking lots as well as cathedral altars, it affirms computer terminals as much as rose gardens and mountain streams, it treats the molecules of the proud politician no differently from those of the penitent saint. It adds a new dimension to the psalmist's declaration, 'The earth is the Lord's, and everything in it, the world, and all who live in it' (Psalm 24:1).

For God's people it means that we will feel at home in the world, recognising Christ permeating and at work in every-thing around us, claiming his inheritance bit by bit. We will want to join with him, affirming his redemptive work in our homes, our workplaces and our communities. All our work will be full-time service. Christ is glorified in a successful busi-ness deal; he is even at work in a failed one. The mission purpose of God is served in a well constructed wall, in a repaired motor car, even in that British habit of coming second in sports events! No door will be considered closed to us, because Christ is already there, inviting us to join him in his ministry. No work will be considered too great or too menial. Only evil will be alien to us, only sin repugnant; yet we will not hide from it in cosseted cloisters. Rather we will engage redemptively in human suffering as Christ does, caring, working for political justice and social regeneration as neces-sary and in the sure knowledge that God is working his purpose out in us and through us until the earth is 'filled with

...ge of the glory of the Lord, as the waters cover the
...kkuk 2:14). Or, as Jesus put it, 'Your kingdom
...ur will be done on earth as it is in heaven.'

Motives matter

The mission of God challenges us to wake up to our calling;
it also invites us to examine our motives. Why should we want
to reach people with the gospel? Are we just trying to sell Jesus
for our own benefit like religious scalp collectors boasting of
their conquests? Is it because we want our church to grow and
to earn a name for ourselves? Is it because our leaders want
the kudos and prestige of a successful work?

It's a common enough motive, if seldom put so bluntly, and
there is something faintly obscene about it, a whiff of the
locker room. Leaders seldom ask what denomination you
belong to – that is akin to enquiring about the colour of your
skin – but sooner or later in conversation about church they
will murmur the question, 'And how big is yours?' I am
always tempted to answer, 'It's not how big it is but what you
do with it that counts!' Or, because of my work with the
regional church, to reply, 'Ninety-five thousand.'

Rapacious competitiveness for large numbers is a base
motive for serving God, especially when the numbers on the
church roll and the bums on Sunday seats is almost entirely
immaterial to our ability to transform the nation. The love of
God is the only acceptable motive for spreading the message
of salvation. Our hearts must be stirred by the fact that so
many people are living without the saving knowledge of
Christ, alienated from the reality of God in their lives, missing
the comfort of the Holy Spirit and the means of grace, failing

to give God his due glory and praise in their lives, and ultimately on their way to some kind of Christless eternity. They are sheep without a shepherd: the field is sour and muddy, the grass is sparse, many are sick and maimed, and the wolves lurk in the undergrowth. Surely the love of Christ should move us to do something about it.

So, what now?

- Consider the purpose of the church you attend. How does it measure up to God's mission purpose?
- Meditate on your personal world, the people, your surroundings, what you do. Review your attitude to it all in the light of this chapter.
- Pray the Lord's Prayer and focus on 'Your kingdom come'. What do you include, and what do you exclude from that petition?

2

The Crazy Farm

Imagine a farmer and his workers with fields of fertile land stretching out before them, and the farmer instructing his workers to gather once a week to polish the tractors and decorate the barn. Having done this, coffee is provided and the workers, with the farmer in the driving seat, then proceed to rev up the tractor for an hour. Very satisfied with the event, relishing the noise and the fumes, the farmer invites his workers to come back again next week and repeat the process. In fact, he promises that this time he will switch on the headlights as well. Everyone is very excited at the prospect.

This process is repeated year on year. The barn becomes ever more comfortable and the tractor positively gleams. So pleased is everyone that a good number meet several times a week to do variations on the revving of the tractor theme. Some of them have even purchased mini tractors and they rev them in their homes, inviting one another to participate in the ritual.

The fields lie barren. On this farm it takes all the time and money simply to keep the barn in good order. Things get even busier when farmers start meeting together, and before you know it they are finding the biggest barn they can and bringing all their tractors together for a grand celebratory rev up. (Perhaps that's why they sometimes call these farmers revs!) The people who fill the barns love these big barn events and some proclaim them harvest gatherings, ignoring the fact that all they are growing is pot plants from the stored seed from a long time ago; so much so that many barns are now into the third generation of pot plant descendants. Genetic mutation caused by inbreeding is rife and freaks are not uncommon.

Occasionally, a seed or two blows in through an unnoticed crack in the barn. If it is harvested it is added to the stockpile of preserved seed. Hopefully, it can be crossed with another preserved seed to produce more pot plants and ease for a while the curse of inbreeding.

Few escape from this barn. Once in a while a maverick seed of the genus *evangelicus* does find a way out and takes a look at the fields. He tells people that they must join him and try to reap some of the wild wheat that he has spotted among the weeds. Most are unwilling to do so and sooner or later the evangelist leaves the barn altogether and goes to work for a para-barn.

All the while the weeds grow and the ground hardens, and even if the farmer were to urge people to get some more seed into the barn he would be met with stout resistance, so daunting is the task. The vast majority simply focus on polishing the tractor and decorating the barn ever more assiduously rather than face the unnatural challenge of the field. So they have been trained, so they have been led, so they will behave.

I hardly have to tell you that sooner or later everyone dies and the barn closes down.

Any farmer behaving like that deserves all he gets. Farms exist for the fields, not for the barn. The barn has its uses, but only insofar as it serves the needs and interests of the fields. If it becomes an end in itself then the end really is nigh!

Most churches in the West are barn-focused models. It isn't difficult to see the clues.

- Typically, we still think the people of the world should come to us, but they don't want to and we can't understand why.
- We rejoice when the world gets the crumbs off our table as though that were the main course: if we get a couple of sentences of genuine gospel on our public media we think the tide is changing and that it must have made a real impact. Frankly, it hasn't.
- We engage in periodic evangelistic missions, often motivated by guilt or the desire to grow a larger congregation.
- We define ministry in terms of in-house activity and measure success by our ability to resource the barn.
- We pray for revival, expecting that it will happen in our meetings.
- We treat gleanings as though they were the harvest. A few converts a year, some of them a late fruiting of Sunday school fifty years ago, do not constitute a harvest. You only get a harvest when you have done the work in the field to warrant it.

This latter is a fundamental, non-negotiable principle. What you sow, you will reap. No gardening, no garnering. Why then do we pray for a revival, for a great harvest to mark the end of the age? Why preach about a great ingathering of souls? Surely we are as self-deluded as a manufacturer of washing machines who 'just believed' in mega-sales of his product without ever advertising his product or setting up the logistics for shipping it out, or even researching his market. He may shout as loud as he likes at his staff, he may whip them up to a veritable frenzy of expectation, he may urge them to imagine every home with one of their machines and call them to wait in expectancy, but not a single machine will leave the factory floor.

Typical evangelism is some of us going out there to get some of them to come in here.

So barn-focused are we that evangelism when it does take place is totally disconnected from the realities of people's lives. As writer and community worker Sue Relf puts it, 'Typical evangelism is some of us going out there to get some of them to come in here to join us in what we are doing in here.' Most of these forays are non-relational, often motivated by guilt, and are antisocial and compromised. I no more want salesmen for Jesus on my doorstep of an evening than I want double glazing salesmen, and as for the offensiveness of somebody shouting at me on a street corner to tell me that I am an evil and wicked person . . . well! Not surprisingly the so-called Decade of Evangelism decayed and by the end of the 1990s the church in England had shrunk by 22 per cent. No farmer or businessman would have been surprised at such a result given the way church operates.

Factory farming for internal consumption

Barn-centred churches define ministry in terms of in-house programmes, and success is measured typically by the ability to resource the barn activities. Seldom does anyone measure success by the ability to fulfil a neighbourhood or field purpose. Tell people that the church is meant to be for the benefit of its non-members and most will nod, but they will behave as though that were not true.

Indeed, the very leaders we hire for this barn-centred purpose, the pastors and ministers, are taken on mainly to look after the barn-dwellers. In our best moments we hope they will discover a neighbourhood, but most church leaders are so pre-occupied with internal care and administration that they miss it. Such leaders soon become slaves to the needs of their dependent members, serving consumer-led programmes that have no significant impact on the world around them. Talk to them about there being other sheep not of the fold, suggest that they are to pastor the entire neighbourhood, and these sheepish shepherds will groan with despair and tell you that they are busy enough already. It is sad to see good men and women with a real vision for serving the community enter church leadership and within a short while become so taken up with committees and meetings and denominational expectations that they entirely lose the very thing that first led them into the ministry.

The reality of our current *modus operandi* is that the majority of church leaders finish up as hirelings set on a career path of their own ambitions, serving a barn for a season before moving on to a bigger and better one. The average tenure is just five years. Whole theologies of 'a call' have been constructed to justify this folly. Recently while on holiday we read of a local church leader who had revived a dying congregation and tapped into a potentially rich source of young people's outreach. It had taken around five years. So what did he do? He moved on to a bigger church! Result: the work goes into paralysis and probable decline, and he never gets to see any fruit, since it takes a minimum of five years' investment with young people before you can expect any lasting return. And the poor church secretary writes plaintively: 'We just know that God already has his new man out there for us. All we have to do is pray and wait.' Tragic.

Just how many church leaders do you know who are where they are because God called them to a field that they feel committed to serving long-term, using the church as God's anointed instrument to do so? Compare that to the number who feel called to a congregation until something better comes along, or things have screwed up so badly that moving on seems the best option.

Rather than face the challenge of the field, it is easier for us to provide an all-round, meet-every-need-of-the-barn-members'-lives programmatic structure. All you need is a hired leader with good managerial skills and a pleasant personality who is not too boring in the pulpit. No history, no future, just endless repetition of the introverted present. An army marking time until it has worn a hole so deep that it vanishes from the landscape. A macabre theatre performing the same play for the same pasty-faced audience, world without end, while the real world rolls by outside. A hospital where the only patients are the staff trapped in an infection-laden institution of their own making. A farm wilfully keeping its fields as set-aside in a time of famine.

So, what now?

- What has the greater priority in your life: the quality of the meetings of your church or the impact of your godly presence in the world?

- What have been the spiritual priorities of your life and the life of your church over the past year? How well do these compare with God's mission purpose?
- How do you rate your leader's long-term commitment to the field around you?
- What percentage of your church neighbourhood do you estimate has heard the gospel so thoroughly that they know it as well as you do?

3
Cultural Aliens

Given the prevailing mentality of the average church, is it any surprise that we who work in the real world, who have families that include many unsaved people, who belong to sports and social clubs, find it difficult to connect our faith with the reality of other people's lives? The in-barn approach nurtures a culturally alien identity. So much so that if an alien from another star system were to land in Britain today and begin to speak about her faith from the perspective of her own culture, she could hardly do worse than the average Christian. To put it bluntly, we sound weird.

It is hardly surprising. Those who educate us in our faith live largely in an artificial world themselves. Their language is that of the ghetto, an odd dialect spoken in a quaint idiom, often using a funny voice laden with code words that few really understand. Try repeating the average sermon or Bible study to your neighbour and you'll see what I mean. Stir in a few cultural taboos of our own making, add some incomprehensible music to accompany bad poetry, wear blinkers to avoid eye contact with all but

your special clique, and you have the perfect, totally irrelevant subculture.

Out of touch, out of mind

If you don't believe me, ask why it is that even the most superficial survey of British culture reveals that the church has no
relevance to the vast majority of the population. People queue
up to watch a film, get into a night club or watch a football
match. They do not queue to attend church. Why not? What
has so shifted in our culture? Why has the church lost its
public appeal when once upon a time people were prepared to
attend in great numbers? The church is irrelevant to most
people. It is a dying and outmoded relic of a previous world,
its theology rendered obsolete by both science and new age
spirituality, and its *modus operandi* is as obsolete as a wind-
up gramophone. Few will mourn or even notice its passing.
Churches close weekly and declining figures for Sunday attendance are reported with gleeful gloom by our media, confirm-
ing what everybody knows: church has passed its sell-by date.
Roman Catholic archbishop Cormac Murphy–O'Connor
declared recently that Christianity is almost vanquished from
these islands. Few would disagree with him.

- We are fast approaching a situation where less than 2 per
  cent of unchurched people under thirty-five have a sufficient Judaeo–Christian God framework to enable them to
  grasp the meaning of the gospel as we usually present it.
- Politically, the church is a part of the declining 15 per cent
  of society classed as traditional and deemed by politicians
  as irrelevant for all practical purposes.

- Most people under fifty have never been to Sunday school.
- The majority of people in Britain have never heard the gospel in a coherent manner and almost all have received a badly distorted view of the faith from school and the media.
- Few people today would consider the church to be a source of spirituality.

Let's face reality: in the West we no longer scratch where people itch; our programmes and our presentations, our style and our services do not connect with the needs of the society around us. We live in a post-gospel, not to say pagan, world where the majority of people have about as much interest in the life of the church as they do in the activities of the local flower arranging club.

Who in our culture goes to hear a speech lasting forty-five minutes, preceded by something as uncool as community singing?

It is time we woke up to the fact that the world is not interested in our programmes, however interesting we might think they are. Some of us think we preach very relevant sermons, but even when we advertise the fact, people don't come. Why should they? Who in our culture goes to hear a speech lasting forty-five minutes, especially when it is preceded by something as uncool as community singing? Let's be honest: the whole concept of a church service, even a so-called modern one, is culturally passé, and yet we invest our best resources, the majority of our budget and considerable time in making this the highlight of our week. If the statistics are to be believed, even the faithful are bored and can't be bothered to come.

Michael Moynagh, in his book *Changing World, Changing*

Church,[1] notes that in 1979 5.4 million people attended church regularly in England each Sunday. By 1998 that figure had dropped by 1.7 million and many of the remaining 3.7 million attend only once or twice a month. At the present rate of decline we are only a few years away from the point where church is no longer a viable presence in our society. To go into the ministry is in prospect a bad career choice.

Of course it's not all bad news. We do have some modest successes. We meet the needs of most of our offspring – though that is waning – and of some of the socially deprived in our society. There are successful churches. Take a train into our inner cities and you'll find white churches failing but you'll also find ethnic churches flourishing. Travel out to the suburbs and provincial towns and you'll discover middle-class evangelicalism looking after itself very nicely, thank you very much. There are inner-city success stories too. New churches do get planted in urban development areas, on university campuses, in socially deprived areas . . .

The evangelist in one Anglican diocese told me that a survey of the churches revealed that 50 per cent were growing rapidly and 50 per cent were dying rapidly. That sounds remarkably encouraging compared to some denominations where the decline is terminal and there are not even enough ministers to go round. Yet such figures belie the truth.

Looking at it optimistically, the history of the church is like the sea: a constantly moving mass of swells and troughs. Most congregations experience both the highs and the lows during the course of their life. Renewal movements come and go. One church dies out but another takes its place and the disaffected

---

[1] Monarch, 2001

find fresh impetus in their new setting. So what's the problem? The problem is this: regardless of the state of your particular church or denomination at this time, be it on a high or in a low, overall the tide is going out and it is doing so at an alarming rate. Furthermore, it is retreating from the young, leaving them – children, teenagers, most people under thirty-five – well and truly beached. In truth, the most successful churches are losing the battle, and the rest of us are doing even worse!

Ghetto churches

How you respond to this will depend on the current state of your own church. Most of us are rather selfish; if we like what we've got then we see no problem. You may be in a dying church but be quite blind to the fact. You like your little club with all its ancestral ties, its familiar old furniture and equally old faces. You find comfort in the weekly rituals and social gatherings. Only despair would make you close down and you will not despair; you will go down fighting, and when your denomination makes the decision that you are no longer viable, you will all too conveniently blame head office for its lack of faith, lack of vision and lack of resources. It will not alter the fact that you close down. Indeed, you probably closed down as a dynamic presence in your community years ago and you didn't even notice the fact. Probably you blamed the declining numbers on the advent of television, or the loss of moral leadership in government, or the education system. Anything or anybody but yourselves.

Your church may be alive and well with a decent sized congregation and all the trimmings. Most towns can boast at least one or two of these and cities a good few more. The members of such churches perhaps understandably relish their relative success, their all-round programme, doctrinal purity, modern worship, good preaching, youth programme and innovative home groups. Some of these churches like to call themselves resource churches, believing that if they gather sufficient strength they can help less viable causes. It seldom happens. Indeed, all that most of the so-called successful churches do is bleed the remaining life out of lesser causes and grow fat. Be warned: there are fewer and fewer small causes for you to feed off and unless something changes you too will begin to starve. The days of your gluttony may be over sooner than you think!

Ghetto churches come in two forms. The first is small, ageing, outmoded and introverted. Ask the members what are its main values and they will answer stolidly: tradition and truth. These are ancestrally dominated churches that perpetuate themselves by reliance on natural progeny and the immediate friends of their progeny to replace those who die. Their shelf life is very limited.

The second type at first sight looks more promising. It is sizeable, middle class, comfortable and family-centred. They will tell you that the main values are worship and fellowship. They even engage in occasional evangelistic forays to get more people to join them in what they are doing in the building. Such churches have often established themselves by seducing the disaffected and the circulating sensation-seekers from other churches with promises of revival, miraculous personal wholeness and emotional fulfilment. They will fade out faster than they think.

The members of these ghetto mentality churches constitute no more than 5 per cent of the population of this nation, and virtually all the Christianity of the Western world operates in this mode at present. For this reason, no significant spiritual revival – and by significant I mean it has transformed a society – has occurred in a modern secular state, nor has any evangelistic strategy succeeded among the 85 per cent of the population that is not already predisposed towards religion. This is a tragic state of affairs and it will get worse unless we change our ways.

Consider your ways

For too long we have concealed the reality of the crisis with the busyness of our diaries. Like Maintenance Martha (Luke 10:38–42) we are so busy preparing meals that Jesus never ordered that we don't have time or energy to hear what he really wants. Mission Mary at least listened to the Master's voice and she came to understand his real purpose – nothing less than the gospel being proclaimed to every single person in the world (Matthew 26:13 refers to this Mary).

The prophet Haggai, during the time of the restoration of Israel to its native land, challenged God's people to consider their ways (Haggai 1:3–11). They like us were busy, preoccupied with their own needs and affairs, yet however hard they worked nothing succeeded. The reason was simple: what they thought was urgent in their economy was not really important in God's. He had a purpose in the rebuilding of the temple that was a whole world away from their personal or even corporate survival – 'the desire of all nations will come, and I will fill this house with glory' (Haggai 2:7). It was time not just for a change of priorities but for an entire change of outlook. The messianic expectation was not just for the nation of Israel but for the blessing of the whole world. The church must likewise awake to its real calling.

However radical the implications, we need to examine ourselves and our work in the light of God's purposes. It is a
dictum of management consultancy that an operation is perfectly designed for the results it is currently producing. If you
want a different result then you must redesign the operation.
We need not only a scheme for reviving our bit of the church;
we need a wholesale, non-partisan movement across the entire
body of Christ, and the responsibility for that lies squarely and
urgently with its leadership and with every one of us.

It is time to consider our ways.

So, what now?

- How well do your church's sermons and group studies
  connect to the everyday world? Could you share the
  content with fellow students or work colleagues?

- What percentage of your church culture and style do you
  think the world around you would feel comfortable and
  familiar with? Think about music, teaching style and language, times of meeting, dress codes, architecture and
  decor, social status, age, location.

- Find out how many people there are in your church with
  no previous church attendance for at least five years before
  they came to yours. Compare that to those who grew up in
  church and those who moved in from other churches.

4

Pity the Battered Bride

Christ may love the church but the world certainly doesn't. A recent survey demonstrated that church was the last place people would go if they had a problem. The media consistently glory in our scandals but rarely report our strengths. Academics distort our history and attack us with venom. Their pundits and prophets give us little more than ten years before we are rendered obsolete by secular humanism, alternative spirituality, religious pluralism, consumerism and sheer indifference. The more sympathetic view us with nostalgic sadness. Buffeted by overwhelming forces they see the church staggering along like a drunken old woman, mocked and avoided because of the tragedy of her life. Torn apart by internal strife, deeply compromised in conduct, desperately clutching at the crumbling edges of her identity, losing money, friends and influence, she inhabits a world of increasing illusion and paranoia and soon even her reason will depart. What went wrong? What brought her to such a wretched state? People shake their heads and move on.

Long years in the ghetto have created an identity crisis.

The bride who lost her way

There is some truth in it: the bride of Christ does seem unsure of her future, and instead of getting on with her marriage preparations she is wandering round the block wondering who she really is. Long years in the ghetto have created an identity crisis.

- Many have lost confidence in their beliefs, and struggle to take the Bible seriously. Their God is reduced to the sum of human nature idealised in a Jesus concept. His death and resurrection are no more than a mythical wish fulfilment, and the Holy Spirit is just good psychic energy. Religious psychobabble for pseudo-intellectuals!
- Even those who retain their classic Christian orthodoxy struggle to make serious sacrifices for their beliefs, and that suggests a deeper and unarticulated doubt. Lack of certainty produces a lot of muted fear in the church, but it trumpets its complaint loudly when we are asked or challenged to go public with our faith. We are suddenly too busy, called to intercede, denying it's our ministry, concentrating on our devotional life, devoting time to the family, pressured by work. Anything but share the gospel that we claim to believe. The silence of the lambs is deafening!

  The silence of the lambs is deafening!

- Most church people are sold out on self-interest. The average congregation is run by no more than 20 per cent of its members and most churches struggle to find sufficient workers for their infrastructure, let alone for their outreach. The rest just sit there. Of course, if you could pay me . . . Can't we hire someone? What's the pastor for, anyway? Apathy rules. Leisure is my treasure and I'm not sharing it unless I have to. The children's work leaders of a church many hundreds strong confided in us recently that they struggled to find enough people to help out in the Sunday school. It's not unusual. Dump the kids, I want my worship and my sermon. Why do you think I put money in the bag?

- We talk about the priesthood of all believers, yet in practice the vast majority of us want to be ministered to rather than to minister. Even those churches that encourage congregational participation in worship find before long that only the same few people actually offer any contribution. The rest of us are too tired, too distracted, too bored, too inadequate. Let the professionals and those who can do the leading, I come here to be fed and I don't much like the idea of a self-service canteen, let alone being expected to peel the vegetables and do the washing-up afterwards! Called to serve. Yes, well, I've got enough on my plate already trying to pay the mortgage and feed the kids and service a reasonable lifestyle.

- This identity amnesia leads to a loss of holiness. Even in such fundamental matters as marital fidelity the church is failing as much as the world, and those churches that claim the soundest doctrine appear to fare no better than the rest. Personally, I am sick to death of reading about pervy priests and promiscuous pastors. Yet the problem isn't simply sexual. The sins of consumerism, pride, division, petty jealousy, deceit and slander are rife. Although the average church is nowhere near as bad as the worst of the world, we are a long way from bettering the best of the world. Self-renewal guru, Susan Jeffers, cites as her reason for giving up on church the noticeable absence of God in our houses of worship. Instead, she finds 'prejudice, judgement, anger and exclusion . . . the perfect ingredients for alienation and hostile acts. *A loving God would strongly disapprove!*'[1] Nothing brought myself and the young people's group closer to leaving our church than when a deacon publicly lambasted our pastor in a church meeting. I have met dozens of former church members who lost their faith as young people because of some caustic remark by an older person. These things go deep.

- Add to this the sins of neglect. The church is supposed to challenge the world with a vibrant, transcendent lifestyle that provokes in people a longing for something better. Our love and care, our joy and freedom from anxiety, our prayerful grace, our words of wisdom and insight, our kindness and refusal to retaliate for a wrong done are a distinctively Christ-like contribution to society that we have apparently forgotten. Jeffers goes on to say that if we recovered these graces many who have left the church would eagerly return. She is probably right.

- Feel guilty? There's a lot of unexpressed guilt in the church. It is hidden beneath our activism, our brash claims and our misinterpretations of grace that replace the rules of the world with the rules of the church and call it freedom. Many Christians struggle with their faith but are seldom allowed to say so. Even more wrestle with secret habits and are eaten up with guilt and the fear

The songs are little more than soporific Muzak to soothe us on our way to a cushioned heaven.

---

[1] Susan Jeffers, *Embracing Uncertainty* (Hodder Mobius, 2002), p. 200.

of discovery. Who dares say that the services are profoundly boring and irrelevant to everyday life? That the songs are little more than soporific Muzak to soothe us on our way to a cushioned heaven? People fear what their leaders might think or say if they ever articulated the truth. I know a leader who once, in a laudable desire for honesty, told his senior leader about his childhood sexual traumas and the scars they had left on his life. The senior leader prayed for him, but from then on treated my friend as a flawed character and never entrusted him with real responsibility again.

Having said all this, there is good news! Christ loves his church still, even if he doesn't love everything about her. He has continued to outwork his purpose wherever he has found us willing, and though there are matters that cause us grief, there are others that fill us with hope for the future.

The gospel has survived intact and undiminished

The sustained intellectual attack on the Christian faith has failed to destroy it. From the late nineteenth century onwards almost everything that can be done to undermine the integrity of the Bible has been tried. Archaeologists, historians and theologians have questioned its historicity, but to no avail; the case for the Bible's historical veracity is stronger than ever and every succeeding discovery has only served to reinforce that fact.

Sceptical professors of theology have tried to discredit and to explain away the miraculous and to deny the possibility of a knowable, personal God. All they have done is demonstrate that they are themselves locked into an outmoded Enlightenment paradigm that makes all their arguments self-defeating.

Rule out the possibility of God at the beginning and you will inevitably prove your own case. It's like saying, 'I believe that humans can't see apples. Therefore, what humans think are apples before their eyes must be an illusion, a government plot, a superstition. The fact that these mythical apples appear to nourish those deluded humans who eat them only shows the power of wish fulfilment!'

Situation ethicists tried to reverse the truth that God is love by seeking to turn love into a god. It has failed to deliver anything more than social confusion and moral despair. Moral relativism has not improved on the foundational moral and ethical principles of the Scriptures, and we are paying the price for the experiment.

Thankfully, after over a century of this nonsense, the majority of Christians in the world today remain firmly and intelligently persuaded of the historic truths of their faith, and globally there are more of us than ever! Look for a shining, captivating truth among the debris of modernism and the rubble of liberalism and you will find this transforming gospel of God's grace diamond sharp and as brilliant as ever.

The Holy Spirit has revitalised our relationship with God

Something quite dramatic happened during this same period of time. The Holy Spirit became a living reality in the lives of believers on a scale scarcely seen since the dawn years of the church. First, with the beginnings of the Pentecostal movement at the start of the twentieth century, came a realisation that the spiritual gifts were still as available and relevant today as they were at the beginning, and ordinary believers could be anointed with heavenly power. Nor need this lead to any downplaying of the Bible; the Pentecostal denominations have proved to be among the most passionate believers in the authority, completeness and integrity of the Scriptures.

The second wave began to occur some fifty years later in what became known first as the neo-pentecostal movement and later the charismatic movement. The impact of the second wave has touched every denomination, both in revitalising worship and devotion to God and also in empowering believers to live and speak for Christ with a fresh joy and vitality. Although the charismatic movement is now over in terms of its existential cultural expression, the rediscovery of life in the Spirit and the reality of spiritual gifts as tools for life and witness continues apace. In recent years it received a fresh boost in what became known as the Toronto Blessing, and the fruits of that are only just beginning to be realised.

The church has rediscovered the meaning of true fellowship

One of the fruits of the charismatic movement has been a fresh understanding of the nature of the body of Christ. Few would want to argue today that the church is essentially the building that Christians use as their local branch headquarters. The church is people, the eucharistic community of faith worshipping, loving, witnessing and serving together.

The grass-roots movement of the laity has achieved a level of unity that the ecumenical movement desired but found itself unable to deliver. Perhaps one of the most vibrant manifestations of this *koinonia* (fellowship) has been the phenomenal growth of home groups. These were virtually unknown outside of young people's 'squashes' when I was a young believer. Today more often than not a regular communicant will be part of a group that meets weekly in somebody's home rather than in the church building.

It has begun to enter another exciting phase as churches increasingly begin to discover that believers in other traditions and denominations are their brothers and sisters in Christ and that there really is only one body of Christ. This unity is not centralised or codified; it is real, local and has enormous potential. As a Benedictine monk put it to me, 'This is a unity not grounded in trying to agree on the detail of our creeds but on the reality of *koinonia* and *kairos* [timeless time, a touch of eternity] in Christ.'

Some years ago I participated in a prayer walk from Edinburgh to London. One of the abiding memories for me was the discovery that God had his people in places where he was not supposed to have them! Labels and places that my most recent affiliations had declared dead proved to be full of life after all. It opened my eyes to the potential of this diversity in unity in local contexts to transform the whole nation.

The church has become again an instrument of mercy

Thirty years ago, when I began to stress the ethical agenda and to insist that we believers must engage ourselves with biblical answers to the great issues of the day, many thought I was quite nuts. Some seriously considered the whole idea a distraction from the central ministry pillars of gospel preaching and devotional instruction. They ignored the fact that the ethical agenda is central to the gospel since it engages us with the pain and dilemma of human existence and the pathos of the cross.

At that time the church was weak in areas of social involvement, and this was especially true of the evangelicals. The liberal social gospel had stressed works rather than faith, and evangelicals had reacted to the point where they had become distanced from the realities of the great moral, ethical and social needs around them.

All that has changed. Today any church leader worth his salt regularly teaches a biblical perspective on the big social, moral and political issues of the day, and many churches are involved in running social action and other mercy ministry activities. Indeed, the Christian work-force is the largest voluntary movement in the country and if we withdrew our labour and goodwill the nation would probably collapse overnight. Our contribution to the national economy alone is worth billions.

Take, as one example, a converted drug addict whose pastor told me she used to steal £150 a day to feed her habit. The church has saved the community in excess of £5,000 per annum, to say nothing of the costs involved should she have been arrested and sent down. Multiply that by hundreds of thousands of people who, in all the diversity of their human need, the church cares for daily.

The church is praying for revival

People are praying again! Church leaders are praying together in villages, towns and cities across the land, laying down their differences to seek God for an outpouring of the Spirit on the nation – and Britain is at the forefront in this! Great prayer movements have risen up, reminding, encouraging and facilitating God's people to pray for revival, for their communities, for the spread of the gospel.

The inspiration for much of this prayer has come from overseas, for one of the greatest phenomena of the twentieth century was the fact that Christianity became truly a global faith. Indeed, we should no longer describe it as a Western religion at all, for the majority of numbers, the greatest expressions of vitality, are found in the emerging world, and that is profoundly reshaping both the theology and practice of the church worldwide. It is their spirituality and their sense of mission that is inspiring churches in the West to believe that God could do something in our own lands.

Although it is true to say that most Christians have only the haziest idea what constitutes revival and many still do not understand the other dimensions involved, the signs are incredibly hopeful. History may not repeat itself, but whenever God's people have cried to him in their time of need he has answered them.

None of this is accidental; it is God's intention that his Son will be glorified in every nation, including our own. The challenges of the twenty-first century are not too great for the Lord, nor need they be so for his people. We stand on the threshold of a prophetic moment when if we take the right steps it is possible to ensure that every man, woman and child in our society can be thoroughly evangelised and every sphere of life touched with the transforming power of the gospel in our lifetime.

Ezekiel 37:1–14 records the astonishing vision of the valley of dry bones. The bones come together, flesh returns to them, then Ezekiel prophesies and the breath of God enters them and they arise as a great army. We are at such a time of revitalisation. An awakening has begun, but it must not stay in the graveyard or it will suffocate once again. Only a radical paradigm shift can save us. What follows is pivotal to the future of the gospel in our land.

So, what now?

- Review your own part in the sins and failings of God's people. Take honest steps of repentance before the Lord.
- Check that you have kept up with what Christ has been doing among his people over recent years. Ensure that you catch up in any area where you lack.
- Read Ezekiel 37:1–14 and allow God to speak faith into your heart until you know that the bones can live.

5

Turned Inside Out

Whatever the supposed glories of our Christian past in Britain or Western Europe – and that really does depend upon where you stand – these nations today are for all practical purposes a pioneer mission field, a world dominated by secular humanism and popular paganism. Unfortunately, most churches have operated for too long on the misapprehension that this is not the case.

Now time is running out. Church attendance is falling all the time and is now down to less than 1 per cent in many places and seldom exceeds 5 per cent almost everywhere else. Whatever residual folk belief in Christianity remains, whatever revival of spiritual interest is currently taking place, the stark fact is that most of the population do not know the Christian gospel because the church operates in a setting and in a manner that fails to touch the real lives of the communities around them. It is not that people are necessarily anti-Christian; they are simply ignorant of the truth because no consistent context exists in their lives whereby they might receive it. Jesus said, 'You will know the truth, and the truth

will set you free' (John 8:32). If this be so then it is a flagrant
denial of human rights to keep people in ignorance. They have
a right to hear the gospel, and God's people, whether we like
it or not, whether it is convenient, comfortable or otherwise,
have a primary responsibility to ensure that they do.

Making a paradigm shift

We need nothing less than a fundamental paradigm shift and
in the future there will be a strong differentiation between
those churches and leaders that have made the shift and those
that have not. Indeed, those that don't make the shift probably have no future. The best they can hope for is to mark time
while slowly sinking into the clay. In all probability they will
be overwhelmed by the waves of change and simply drown,
and sooner than they think. It is not even a choice between
revival or survival. We must change our perspective or perish
and with our perishing will go the spiritual hopes of the
nation!

What do we mean by a paradigm shift? A paradigm, in this
context, is an assumed model of reality upon which we uncon-
sciously base all our decisions and activities. I am blessed to
be in a marriage paradigm that grants me both the benefit and
the responsibility of taking my wife into account in all of my
life's activities. It also allows me, with typical and regrettable
maleness, to assume that I will find clean, ironed shirts in my
wardrobe!

Without such paradigms life would be unliveable; we would
need to make a fresh, fundamental analysis of our state of
being before we could perform even the simplest action. Just
suppose, for example, that my paradigm told me that gravity

was unpredictable. I could not take a single step without performing elaborate calculations more usually reserved for rocket science.

Not surprisingly, the consequences of a paradigm shift, a change in the fundamental assumed model, can be far-reaching. In the second century AD Greek humanist astronomer Claudius Ptolemy proposed that the earth must be the centre of the universe – a logical deduction from the humanism of Hipparchus, whose ideas he drew on. Despite the almost unworkable mathematics required to chart the movements of the planets and stars, the paradigm held sway for centuries. It took the Christian astronomer, Nicolaus Copernicus, with his theistic view of the cosmos, to propose in the mid-sixteenth century a new paradigm; namely, that the sun is the centre of the solar system. This undoubtedly correct paradigm solved the mathematics and sat well with biblical theology, but it profoundly disturbed the Western establishment. From being the centre of everything, we were now only third rock from the sun. All subsequent philosophy is based on the pessimistic notion that we are lost in space. We are eternally lonely and desperately want to know if there is anyone else out there.

Christian conversion constitutes a far more personal paradigm shift. To call Christ the Lord is to abandon our egocentricity in favour of a theocentric state of being radically outworked in every aspect of our personal and communal lives. Little wonder that the language of devotion speaks of moving from darkness to light, from death to life. One might even call it being born again!

So, what is the paradigm shift required of church leaders and their congregations? Our prevailing paradigm is sometimes called the Jerusalem-type. It assumes that the surround-

ing community has a belief in a Creator, a knowledge of the
Ten Commandments, familiarity with the Jewish sacrificial
system and a messianic expectation, along with a belief in
divinely inspired writings contained in a leather cover and a
commitment to attend a service of worship each Sabbath. It
allowed Peter on the Day of Pentecost to call people to faith
in Christ in the certainty that those listening understood what
he was talking about. These assumptions could be made in our
own society when most people attended Sunday school and
where education systems taught the essentials of the Christian
faith. Those days have passed and that in itself renders the
paradigm redundant.

The Jerusalem-type church is a gathered model. Most
church life is based on the perspective of the holy priest in his
holy place calling people together to receive the holy blessings
from his hand. The building and its activities are the effective
centre of spirituality, sacred space carefully crafted and cere-
monially consecrated. This model has been with us for centuries and in spite of its fundamental flaws did quite well once the
missionaries had left and the state and its local power brokers
enforced church attendance as the norm. It will not suffice in
our post-Christian world where people have no reason to
attend church.

Lest any should be tempted to think that this is a problem
only for the established and sacramental churches, experience
demonstrates that almost all shades of church are based on the
same fundamental paradigm. Just try moving the furniture in
some free churches and you will see what I mean! We are a
far cry from the dynamic free church movements of history, and
today 'gathered' means building-centred, service-centred activities, and in many free and newer churches a new priesthood of

power has arisen, claiming extraordinary anointing to preach and minister to the gathered congregation.

This centralist paradigm is an *in here/out there* model. It sees mission or evangelism as an extension of its gathered life, a form of recruitment rather than the heart of our existence. In practice this means that except for a few special 'full-time' missionaries and evangelists the rest of us have to add recruitment to our already busy leisure time.

Just try moving the furniture in some free churches and you will see what I mean!

It takes very little to see that this model is based on the rarefied perspective of the full-time church leaders. Ordinary Christians live out here in the real world, but if our leaders are immersed in this centralist paradigm their teaching can have little relevance to our ordinary lives. After all, what really matters is turning up at the building for services, attending meetings, putting in voluntary service to church activities, giving money to sustain the whole, and trying to get others in to do the same. The average Christian receives very little help in how to conduct their business, administer the household finances, deal with the kid's education, play better golf or handle a mid-life crisis. Tell me that this is not the business of the church and I will say that your church will soon be out of business. Jesus addressed everyday issues because he lived in the real world, and he expects us to do the same. Faith is not a separate sacred compartment; it is a totality of being in the presence of God.

There is an alternative paradigm and it is sometimes called the Antioch-type church. Antioch-type churches are missionary communities totally engaged in their culture and not relying at all on the Jerusalem assumptions. It is an *out here/in there* model:

the diffused paradigm begins not with an in-here, go-out-there-and-get-them-in mentality, but with an out-here-in-the-market-place-of-life, gather-in-there-when-we-need-to model. It is a model for diffused, mobilised, twenty-four-hours-a-day, seven-days-a-week mission living. Instead of trying to get the world onto our holy turf we sanctify their unholy turf by our incarnational Christian presence, our sensitive proclamation and our eager persuasiveness. All the ground that we stand upon becomes holy, not just because the earth

Ordinary Christians live out here in the real world.

is the Lord's and everything in it, but because we are there, bringing something of the presence of Christ – and that lights the holy fire in our homes, our workplaces and our communities.

In this diffused model the priesthood of all believers takes precedence over the specialised priesthood of the church leaders and it finds expression not simply in a few religious acts such as daily quiet times but in every aspect of life. So I will conduct my business as a priest, I will play soccer with my kids as a priest, I will have a meal out with friends as a priest. Christian service is defined not as an add-on to my life's activities but as those very activities themselves sanctified by the presence and power of God working through me. I discover a new awareness of the glory of the commonplace and I cease to divide my life up between the sacred and the secular. My normal work is full-time service. The real life and witness of the church is seen not in those specialised activities conducted by the few but in the whole lives of the many. We become an incarnational missionary community rather than just a witnessing congregation.

Does this make our buildings and meetings, indeed our clergy, redundant? No more so than the sun being the centre of the solar system makes the earth redundant. What it does do is change the perspective and that has radical implications for how we view our gatherings. So never fear, church leader: God's people will still have good, and arguably better, reasons to gather together!

We will explore more of this and its implications later on. Right now we need to note that Paul's journeying from Antioch led him to Athens. The sermon that Paul preached on Mars Hill, recorded in Acts 17, relied for its effectiveness on none of the assumptions that Peter could make in Jerusalem. Despite his intensely Jewish roots, Paul had to make the transition to intelligent cultural engagement with the pagan world. He did so by drawing on their culture rather than his own, beginning where they were rather than where he had reached. He spoke of universal concerns about religion, superstition, the human spirit, justice and death. His appeal when it came led not to a religious revival meeting but to an intense discussion and exploration of the relevance of Jesus among those who did respond. Paul's approach laid the foundations for the dramatic spread of the gospel among the Gentiles; it also provides us with a model for how to reach our contemporary society based upon the diffused paradigm. The future of the church will lie with those who can make the shift to an Antioch vision and can engage with our present-day Athens.

Wherever I teach this material people nod with apparent understanding, but I have yet to meet more than a handful of folk who have got it in one. This observation leads me to conclude that it really is a matter of divine revelation; the penny has to drop. Typically, those with evangelistic gifts respond full of enthusiasm but they are usually just dreaming up more evangelistic programmes for more people to be badgered into doing. Pastors often go quiet, fearing that their flocks will no longer be cared for and that their ministries will be redundant, even though I assure them that nothing could be further from the truth. Paradigm shift is easy to explain; it is harder to grasp than we first imagine.

Let me help you see which model you are currently working to, beginning with the old centralist model.

- These churches focus on the building and the importance of the meetings. Such churches may well include home groups but these are simply a modification of the gathered model. This is an issue largely unaddressed by those taking the cell church route and, until they do, their cells will never function as they were intended to.
- Under the centralist paradigm people gather to meet God, and the prayers usually give the game away: 'Lord, we pray that you will come and meet with us today.' 'We draw near to your presence.' 'We are standing on holy ground.' I want to ask, 'So where were you before you got here? And where was God?'
- Centralist churches are often strongly front-led by the experts, be they priests, worship leaders or teachers. The majority of the congregation are passive responders. Ministry is deemed to be doing what the leaders do – an appallingly narrow concept of ministry for sure! It is these same leaders who appear to have the monopoly on the anointing of the Spirit, and startling results are sometimes promised when they 'move in their anointing' or perform the sacramental act.
- Under this model faith becomes restricted to a sacred compartment concerned with religious performance and

devotional exercises. Self-preoccupied, we quickly produce dependency cultures served by a constantly tired minority of key workers.

- Evangelism in the centralist model is sporadic and specialist, and often alien to the culture of the people at which it is directed.

Now, by contrast, here are some characteristics of the diffused model.

- The diffused model puts the focus on the people and the quality of their lives in the secular community. Taught to walk with confidence in the world arena, such Christians will keep themselves from the sins of the age but engage fully in the culture. Instead of gathering to meet God, they go out into life to meet God.

- Since every member of a diffused church considers themselves to be full time for Jesus, individual participation in the faith and the mission is high and is outworked in daily life right out here in the world. Ministry is redefined as every believer at every hour and in every place, with all the people aware of the spiritual sowing, nurturing and harvesting role that they play.

Instead of gathering to meet God, they go out into life to meet God.

- When such Christians do meet together they do so as field workers gathering for thanksgiving, prayer, encouragement, running repairs and further training. Outwardly focused, these churches are energy producers rather than consumers.

- Diffused church allows us to do justice to the apostolic

spheres of politics, commerce, arts, media, education, cine, finance and the environment, and is really the only proper expression of kingdom theology. There is no other way that the church can expect to bring God's peace to the nations.

- The diffused church extends the dynamic range of ministry possibilities far beyond the so-called bounds of church life and releases the full potential of what it means to be 'a kingdom and priests to serve our God' (Revelation 5:10). Every-member ministry is no longer a pipe-dream but a daily reality.

- The paradigm shift redefines the object of the leaders' ministry. In most current models of church the members are the object and the leaders spend all their time trying to serve their needs. The diffused model focuses on the world as the object of our ministry, and the church then becomes the instrument to fulfil that object. The task of leadership changes. From now on it is concerned with equipping, enabling, empowering and encouraging the congregation for their ministry to the world. We will see later how we can best facilitate this.

To summarise, by analogy, what the paradigm shift means:

You are a high street clothing store whose customer base has been so whittled away that you now sell only to your own staff. You want to put all your staff into market-stall selling and to recruiting new staff whom you will then ensure are trained to repeat the process.

You are a restaurant that now caters only for its own cooks. You want your cooks in future to prepare food on the customers' own premises and to train those customers in how to make the dishes themselves, so that they in turn can train others.

You are the local general hospital that performs endless medical checks on its own medical staff. You now want that staff to work in the community, bringing health and healing on the spot, and producing further health workers who can do the same.

So, leaders will no longer measure their status by the size of their congregation but by the effectiveness of its mobilisation. If the ministry is all of God's people all of the time and in every place, then we must learn to treat the ministry as *out here* rather than *in here*. The real question becomes, 'How well are your people working for Christ out here in the field?'

- Our abundance of in-house activities can fool us into thinking that we are honouring Christ, but the inescapable implication of kingdom theology is that single mission purpose is the only proper response to the lordship of Christ.
- Leaders may justify their existence by the fullness of their diaries and the eloquence of their sermons, but God assesses us by the degree to which we succeed in equipping the saints for their ministry in the field.
- Believers can settle for leisure time church attendance and avoid sins they probably didn't want to do anyway, but the Lord calls his people to be full-time expressions and instruments of his mission to the world.

All this constitutes a call to honesty and humility, to true faith for the future grown in the soil of spiritual modesty. We can delude ourselves within the proud barns of our ecclesiastical self-interest, but if we stand in the barren fields, sober reality obliges us to consider our ways. In short, this is no less than a call to 'turn to the Gentiles' – an Antioch rather than Jerusalem church mentality at a time when the 'fall of Jerusalem' is taking place brick by brick!

So, what now?

- You and the church you attend are operating in one para-digm or another: gathered or diffused. Examine carefully which one it is.
- If a visiting speaker were to ask all the ministers to stand, would every member instinctively rise to their feet? Would you?
- Do you go to church to meet God or go to work to meet God? Yes, it can be both, but which has the precedent in your life, really?
- As an exercise, describe your ministry wholly in terms of non-church activities. Do you think you have a full-time ministry?

6
Who in the World?

Something changes the moment we make the paradigm shift in our perception of what it means to be God's people. We realise that we have been standing in the mission field all the time. It begins not across the water but across our front doorstep, and for some before that. We are missionaries and we need to understand the field where God has placed us. What is its language and culture? How does it operate as a society? What are its current beliefs and values? How can we make the connections to communicate the gospel and transform such a society? There is undoubtedly a chasm to be crossed between our church culture and the world we inhabit for Jesus.

Visiting a provincial town on a hot summer's evening we watch some church people entering their building proudly displaying its nineteenth-century founding date. Women in dark blue two-pieces dutifully don their dark blue hats, men wearing solemn faces and grey suits cross the sober threshold followed by boys clad in ties and smart jackets. At 6.30 p.m. the featureless brown doors are closed fast – to keep in and to keep out.

The sloppily dressed man tending his garden fence four

doors away ignores them, as they do him. So does the trendy young woman returning to her live-in boyfriend in the flat three doors away. A cosmic gulf exists between them and the religious fashions and scruples of the nineteenth-century British Empire.

The world has changed. In that same road a family has returned from a pleasant day by the sea. Three guys are watching football on Sky and are just into the first round of six-packs. A teenage clubber is deciding how much flesh she should reveal in the nightly competition to get lucky. Six years into marriage a couple with a young baby are having a row over money. Down the road a computer geek watches a porno video on ADSL while the retired pair next door are preparing to take the dog for a walk.

The days are gone when the world and his uncle went to church after milking time. Fine points of doctrine no longer form a supper-time conversation. Nowadays the world frankly couldn't care less!

Yet the Christian bit doesn't quite go away. Witness the people entering cathedrals after the death of Princess Di, the increased congregations following September Eleven, or the response to the tragic murders of Holly Wells and Jessica Chapman in Soham. People go to church in times of sorrow. Still.

But it's ruled out of the public debate and the public consciousness. Religion has been officially privatised and church is reduced to a consumer choice like Tesco's or Sainsbury's – except that while we must eat daily, we attend church like a visit to the dentist. Only when it hurts or, if we are dutiful, for a six-monthly check-up. Those who visit the dentist every week are either rather sad or they have very bad teeth.

So if our world is no longer consciously Christian, what is it instead? A mission field, for sure – here, right on our doorstep – but what kind of mission field? Here are some pen portraits to help us understand the society that God wants to transform through our witness and influence.

Three generations of misbelief

Generation one

Arthur Smith was sixteen when the Second World War started. Well educated though inexperienced, he found himself conscripted as a junior officer and in 1940 he was sent to France to lead a detachment of men. The mission was a disaster; his troops were ambushed and many were killed. Out of ammunition and terrified for their lives, the remnant skirted the northern coast of France in the hope of reaching England. They were saved at Dunkirk.

Arthur survived the war but never forgot his experiences nor the fact that the God of Sunday school failed to answer his prayers. He put his trust in science instead. That and that alone held the key to the future. He went on to apply scientific principles to business and did well. He was a survivor – tough, self-made, unsentimental – and convinced that through the triumph of science and medicine over superstition and ignorance the world would evolve into a better place.

Talk to Arthur about God and he would dismiss you with, 'If you had seen what I saw during the war . . .' Not that he refused to attend church for the hatching, matching and dispatching rituals of his family and friends; that was all part of being English and respectable, and Arthur was certainly that. But the beliefs failed to convince him. Propositions would have to be proved and proved scientifically for him to change his mind. No one ever succeeded in doing so.

Arthur developed cancer in later life and was nursed by his Christian daughter-in-law. She was not the nursing type and clearly found it hard going. He appreciated her sacrifice and the love she displayed. Cynical as he was, something melted in his heart. As a result I had the privilege of leading him to Christ just before he died. There are hundreds of thousands of Arthurs waiting to be reached. All of them are over sixty.

Generation two

The hem of Mary Peters' skirt and the hang of her ethnic beads met somewhere north of mid-thigh. Late-sixties London was swinging and the Beatles and the Stones provided the anthems of freedom. Comprehensively well educated, politically left wing, she discussed Sartre, read D.H. Lawrence and Simone de Beauvoir, and tried desperately to *be*. So Mary hung out, tuned in, dropped out, slept around, tripped out, burned her bra, marched against the Vietnam War, stripped off at Woburn to the sounds of Jimi Hendrix and T-Rex and attended every Happening in the hope that it would. Her world was now; it might not be tomorrow, for overshadowing Mary's world was the Bomb. By the mid-seventies she was a freaked-out laid-back hippie at the weekends and a junior advertising executive inspired by Germaine Greer the rest of the time. By the eighties she had embraced the new technology, got herself a degree in communications skills and was a senior partner in her own agency.

Nowadays she lives with her husband in an expensive house in Oxfordshire, from which she continues to write. Her husband helped develop microwave technology and made a fortune in business by turning existentialist now-ness into consumer instant-ness. Their children are all privately educated. Mary is a vegetarian and calls herself Buddhist. She attends yoga classes and her home is luxurious traditional English with feng shui overtones.

She has met Christians over the years and has attended charismatic services that seemed to touch something deep inside her. She has fallen over, shaken and laughed and willingly believed that it was the power of God that had come upon her. Yet she lacked the staying power and although the church tried to get a commitment from her she proved a frustrating task. Recently, both she and her husband have begun to attend an Alpha course run by local Anglicans.

Generation three

Dave is a computer programmer for a multinational service company. At twenty-seven he drives the regulation BMW and shares a flat with three other blokes when he isn't sleeping over with his current girlfriend, Miranda. She owns her own pad but is often away at European sales conferences.

Dave and his mates spend their time watching football, boozing and surfing the Internet for loony sites. At the weekends they go clubbing and lay silly bets on who will be the first to pull. Each has slept with fewer girls than he boasts but more than he can remember. Holidays are usually to Ibiza. Between them they read *GQ*, *Loaded* and *Maxim* and buy all the fashion accessories for this year's image. Tolerant, guilt-free and confident, they have a lot of fun and plan to make their money now so that they can settle down in their late-thirties and retire by fifty.

Christianity is non-existent in Dave's life and he and his

mates have no language with which to discuss religion. He did watch *The Matrix* though, and it made him think, as has some of the science fiction that he enjoys. Miranda is having an influence on him too. She is psychic as well as sexy and Dave has been on meditation retreats with her a couple of times where they spoke of going back to the future – which ironically made sense to him. Miranda has all sorts of books on the old mysteries, runes and folklore. Dave

The few charismatics he has met seemed to offer no more than middle-aged dreary music while trying to get him into a cell!

has had enough weird experiences to convince him that there is more to life than computer programming.

He describes himself as slightly spiritual and he admires those, like Miranda, who have really got it. There is no way he would associate spirituality with Christianity and the few charismatics he has met seemed to offer no more than middle-aged dreary music while trying to get him into a cell! The one group that did impress him, he met at a Celtic festival. They told him they were followers of Jesus who believed but did not belong to a traditional church. Friendly and thoughtful, they encouraged him to follow his journey towards the Light of the World and wished him well. He might just take up their invitation to meet again.

Josh and Kylie are members of a group of mates who kept together in the local pub after leaving school. Josh is a stores manager for a local garage repair shop and Kylie sells shoes in a discount store. Both live on a local council estate. Their language is Anglo-Saxon and sprinkled liberally with swear words, though they would not recognise them as such, this being their normal idiom. Although they manage their jobs, neither is educated and they are inherently mistrustful of those who are. Although they talk about getting a better life they see that possibility only through winning the lottery and in reality are happy provided they are getting on together.

Josh and Kylie's world is clannish and tribal and strongly matriarchal. Thinking is done out loud and in the group, often very loudly and emotionally. The idea of quiet contemplation is quite alien to them. Loners are viewed with suspicion and children are staunchly defended against all comers. The group is welcoming to its authentic own kind but is deeply critical of the middle classes and what it sees as hypocrisy. As a group they are totally unchurched, consigning church to the dustbin of establishment hypocrisy along with the *Daily Mail* and all government authority. If they do attend a church, for a wedding or funeral, it isn't because of some remnant of folk religion but because they have a sense of theatre and want the opportunity to party.

What others call vices Josh and Kylie call legitimate pleasures. Most of their group smoke heavily and they consume unbelievable amounts of alcohol. They party frequently, dancing non-stop to the latest techno or, on karaoke nights, singing sentimental ballads. They do drugs but not cocaine or heroin. Holidays are at the coastal club hotspots on the Med. Moderation is an unknown concept and they are not protective of their health.

These new barbarians are the most unreached and by far the largest section of the UK mission field.

The humour of this group is bawdy, with the lads pulling each other's legs about masturbation and their success in pulling birds and the girls getting hilarious about the vibrators they purchased at a lingerie party and about planning their next girls' night out to watch male strippers. The girls dress unashamedly sexily on nights out while the guys try to cultivate the art of cool. Sex for all of them is recreational and more to do with scoring than with relational satisfaction. They are more likely to find that watching football together in the pub or when discussing *EastEnders*.

These new barbarians are the most unreached and by far the largest section of the UK mission field. Evangelisation among them has to be incarnational – that is, by Christians living among them, engaging in care-focused social activism and earning their street cred the hard way. Communicating the gospel requires the gifts of raw humour and emotive storytelling and it must be accompanied by miracles and divine healing to have any bite. The only music that will work is the kind that the average church would hate. Nobody has yet bothered reaching Josh and Kylie. Their prospects are not good: they might be lucky and get by if the group holds but they are likely to have debt, health, crime, drug, depression and relational problems as they get older.

These are our three generations, and for those who prefer charts, following is one that broadly summarises these profiles for each age band and the cultural era that has had the biggest effect on them.

God loves them all, and it is his desire that each one should receive the transforming power of the gospel through the witness of his people. They are not aliens; they are the people we live alongside and with whom we share a common heritage. Our one task is to restore the spiritual conversation, and that requires a shift on our part rather than theirs.

Cultural era	1940–1960	1960–1980	1980–
Present age band	over 60	35–60	under 35
Value system	Scientism	Existentialism	Mysticism
Motivation	Survival	Freedom	Meaning
Source of hope	The evolving future	The present event	The authentic past
Maturation	Cynicism	Materialism	Paganism
Christian expression	Liturgical	Charismatic	Celtic
Evangelistic style	Prove the proposition	Prove the power	Prove the presence

So, what now?

- You can probably identify which generation you fit. List all your friends, relatives and colleagues, and mark which generation they belong to. Begin to pray about how they will hear the gospel.
- What do you believe are the key openings for the gospel for these people, beginning from their culture?
- Do these people know that you are a Christian because of the way you try to help their lives or because you spend a lot of time in your church culture?

7
The Present is Past

New-paradigm, revitalised churches are beginning to emerge, but the average church is still a privatised cultural enclave working to a redundant paradigm and attempting outreach across an unbuilt bridge. Such churches as they stand have no hope of fulfilling the mission purpose of God – and it will not get easier. The gap widens by the month as our culture accelerates away from all that old-paradigm churches could once take for granted to sustain their life. Change is mandatory and urgent, or death is inevitable and sooner than we imagine.

Goodbye to history

When Bob Dylan wrote 'The times they are a-changing' he probably had little idea of just how rapid that change would be. Inspired by humanism, fuelled by technology and paid for by advertising, the world is changing at a rate and with a force so great that Leonard Sweet describes it as being caught in a cultural tsunami that will for ever alter our social landscape. Like the man said: the future just ain't what it used to be no more.

The rate and the extent of change is awesome and it leaves some people reeling. Alvin Toffler back in 1970 described the phenomenon as 'future shock' when he tried to analyse our often traumatised response to the world of all-consuming high speed change, but in 1970 life was leisurely compared with today. Now we race frenetically towards a future that has no end, a goal-less evolution towards an undefined tomorrow, and nobody wants to be left behind. But the road is increasingly littered with casualties – burned out, Prozac-soaked, dislocated heroes who didn't quite make it.

Many others thrive on change; the M generation, those whose entire conscious lives are lived out in the dawn years of the third millennium, take change in their stride. For them buttons and mouse clicks hold no fear, only fascination. What will this one do? Where do I want to go today? Netwise, anywhere in the world, and fast. Whatever we make of the future, for many it will be an exhilarating experience, but it will be almost entirely disconnected from history. This is a post-everything world – post-war, post-industrial, post-Christian, postmodern.

When New Labour came to power and systematically began to excise the remaining traces of Britain's imperial past, it reflected the mood of a new millennium characterised by globalisation and transient now-ness. Most senior figures of influence in our society were born after the Second World War and grew up in the cultural revolution of the 1960s. They have no time for the old militarism, rigid conformity and emotional repression of their parents' generation. The irony of actor John Cleese's

Traditional values suit only our folksy desire for nostalgic cameos, like church weddings complete with bells.

famous line 'Don't mention the war. I did, but I think I got away with it' firmly dispatched the old order along with ration books, gas masks and National Service. The wars of the future would be fought by professional soldiers in far away places, with the highlights edited for family viewing on prime time television. Institutions, including churches, that continue wartime values are viewed with incredulity by the majority of under-sixties alive today. Traditional values suit only our folksy desire for nostalgic cameos, like church weddings complete with bells, frills and horse-drawn carriages, or the Last Night of the Proms, but they have no place in everyday life.

Prime Minister Margaret Thatcher's era saw the dismantling of Britain's industrial past and the painful emergence of service and hi-tech industries to replace it. Alvin Toffler's earlier book, *The Third Wave*, points out that industrial society was built around a source code of standardisation, specialisation, synchronisation, concentration, maximisation and centralisation. The post-industrial landscape no longer needs or accepts that code. What then of churches that still operate on the basis of a fixed ritual administered by experts at set times of religious intensity congregated in a special building? When will flexitime reach the morning communion service?

The days when Christianity dominated the political, cultural and intellectual landscape are over. No longer does the state grant tacit power and influence to the church. Even less does the intelligentsia. To study theology is to depart from the mainstream of intellectual life. Active Christianity is now a minority social religion meeting the personal needs of its remaining adherents, a club for the convinced – and so last century! Nobody wants its influence in the realm of public life and few see it as a source of authentic spirituality.

Jesus is a swear word and, for those who get to know anything about him, also a good man, but the church is viewed with distinct distaste by older generations and with total disinterest by the younger. For the first time in history religion is decidedly out for the majority white population, and spirituality has become a matter of individual tailoring to meet my perceived personal need for something transcendent. Just don't try to hedge me or to organise my experiences. I will find my own sacred spaces, but they are unlikely to be in a church building – too creepy, too cold, too drab or just plain locked up at a time when I might venture in. Julia Cameron, in *The Artist's Way*,[1] finds her space in 'a large clock store or a great aquarium', generating as they do for her a sense of timeless wonder. Few would expect to find that experience in a church service.

Nor will our society any longer grant to institutional Christianity exclusive rights to the truth. God may forgive us our trespasses but the world will not forgive us our manifest flaws. We are discredited and will have to take our modest place among all the other contenders for spiritual allegiance in the market-place of religions, and for most people that means, if they bother at all, some sort of pick'n'mix.

This isn't to say that the government and society have no time for the church. They are quite happy to grant us the refuse of modernity. We are more than welcome to exercise our mercy ministry among the dropouts and failures and inadequates of society, especially if we will do it for free, but the world no longer wants our gospel or its radical social implications. Currently the only way to influence policy is to

---

[1] Pan Books, 1995.

remove virtually all of our Christian content to make our offering acceptable to a world dominated by secularism.

The demise of the great institutions of the modern era has created a vacuum that has invited a rush of new but uncoordinated ideas from the fringes. Those fallen institutions and their philosophic values include the church, communism, imperialism, socialism, rationalism and monarchism. The resulting cultural scene is fragmentary and individualistic, a mosaic in motion. No longer is there an agreed big picture. Truth is whatever turns you on, a consumer choice. There are absolutely no absolutes. The spiritual journey is a search for a fuller humanity, not a path to reconciliation with an angry God, and when we die we are simply recycled into the eternal cosmic consciousness. What then of a church that claims to possess a book of truth, or a pope who when he speaks *ex cathedra* is infallible, or a first-century religious Martyr who claimed to be the Truth, let alone you when you stand up on Sunday to preach as 'the oracle of God'?

In the future people will think in terms of cybernetic loops rather than yes/no straight lines.

I tend to side with those who see postmodernism as a period of transition rather than a distinct new philosophy. Yet one factor seems set to remain. In the future people will think in terms of cybernetic loops rather than yes/no straight lines, and that will be problematic for those who see belief systems as fixed and provable propositions as immutable as the Newtonian clockwork universe. If there is to be a theology for the future it will be one that is formed interactively by the dynamics of the participants' lives and not by the pronouncements of the authorities.

Casualties of change

The church along with other traditional institutions may be a casualty of a rapidly changing world, but there are others.

The underclass

One of the phenomena of the late-twentieth century was the growth of the middle classes and arguably it was this that finally discredited communism. The great wealth and accompanying power of the aristocracy had steadily eroded throughout the century, but it was the lifting of so many ordinary people through better health care, improved technology, cheap consumer goods, comprehensive education and affordable home ownership that really made the difference. Remove people's reason for discontent and you remove the threat of revolution. Thus it was possible for Margaret Thatcher to take on the Trade Unions and to break their power simply because the issues at stake were no longer life or death, or even destitution.

However, all is not well and there is in our cities a significant underclass that has missed out on all the benefits of modern life. They live on council estates, they are unemployed, they commit a lot of crime, they use and deal in heavy drugs, most children are in single-parent families, many are depressed and afraid, violence in the home and on the streets is commonplace, alcoholism is rife, health is poor, prostitution is a way of life for many women, car stealing and joy riding by teenagers is a nightly activity. In fact, the underclass poses a threat to all the values so assiduously guarded by those who have made it to the middle classes and there have been serious British academics who have proposed that we should find a way of quietly disposing of the problem that carries sinister undertones of 'a final solution'.

Yet these are people for whom Christ died and they, like their counterparts in other countries, need not only the gospel but social, economic and cultural redemption. One thing is certain: the middle-class church will not reach them from the safety of the suburbs, nor will the gentrified churches in the revived city centres. It will need nothing less than a sacrificial and incarnational Christianity prepared to identify with the poor where they are, to live among them and walk with them, to make up in our bodies what is still to be made up in the sufferings of Christ. For if as we said earlier our theology of the lordship of Christ teaches that he 'fills everything in every way' (Ephesians 1:23) then it teaches us that he fills not only the molecules of joy but the molecules of pain as well; and since the church is the fullness of that same Christ it must surely be prepared to rejoice with those who rejoice but also to weep with those who weep. Tentative steps have been taken through the Eden Project in Manchester in recent times but it will take a major shift in our understanding of church to make a real difference.

Sexual partners, serial scandal

Sexual fidelity is a major casualty of our fast-changing world. The difference between my generation of teenagers and today's is that while mine indulged in sex outside marriage they still felt guilty about it. Today, extramarital sex is commonplace, and there is no guilt.

That is not to say there is no moral code today. Cheating in love is deeply offensive to the current generation, whether within a steady relationship or within marriage itself. Sex is

OK, marriage is OK, living together is OK, but only one at a time, please.

Serial relationships present us with enormous social and personal problems, not least the confusion faced by the relatives of those concerned. Just how many dads should one kid have to have? Where do you go for Christmas Day? Who inherits what in the will? How many more houses will we have to build to accommodate all these people living separate lives? Will children with two genetic parents under the same roof become a new advantaged elite and will that create problems of envy in schools, and will they be victimised by unwise teachers attempting to affirm the less privileged?

Twenty-first-century churches must come to terms with the reality of a variety of family units that do not fit with the traditional interpretation of the biblical norm. Our language must reflect this but at the same time we must raise up a standard against the scandal of our nation's sexual misbehaviour. This poses quite a challenge when a man and a woman come to faith who once were partners but are now in different, and not necessarily married, relationships. They turn up in your church and offer to teach in Sunday school. Their kids are all half-siblings. What do you do?

Then there are those who are onto their third, fourth or fifth relationship. Can you really suggest that they go back to their first marriage, especially when as is likely the original partner has long since moved on to another person? Or do we treat such people as slightly second class – allowed in the church but not open for office? Similarly, do you ask a couple in long-term relationship to separate before they can become Christians, or do you accept them as they are? Established churches have had to revise their practices and no longer treat divorcees, especially the innocent parties, as second rate by merely blessing their remarriage while refusing to actually marry them. There's nothing very tidy about the mission field.

The church has a reputation for judgementalism and repression in matters sexual. People are afraid to seek help from churches because they already feel badly enough about their problems and really can't face another guilt trip. Meanwhile, the demand for marriage guidance counselling has never been higher, as witness the three-month waiting list at many branches of Relate. We are obliged by law to make buildings accessible to disabled people but in this matter it seems we require the maritally disabled to negotiate an assault course before they can get the help they need.

The loss of belonging

There was a time when you knew your roots and your place in a settled community. That has gone for most people with the advent of globalisation.

These words found in Daniel are spot on: 'Many will go here and there to increase knowledge' (Daniel 12:4). We live in a global village, a world where no part is much more than a day's journey away and where we can speak to one another at little short of the speed of light, spreading ideas and information in a depth and variety undreamed of by our forebears. This is the world of global multinationalism, of strategic defence policies that span continents, of international agreements at the UN, of World Bank and G8 summits that affect the lives of billions.

Globalisation has brought widespread job insecurity. Whole industries can be moved to a more convenient nation to reduce the cost of production or distribution and there is little that politicians can do about it. Economic migration follows. Nobody expects a job for life any longer. Few can expect to live in the same area for more than a few years. Churches find it hard to build long-term commitment with those whose outlook is determined by unavoidable job relocation. Leaders may need to offer date-stamped membership as a more viable alternative to a lifetime membership.

Yet for all this global perspective and transitoriness, people crave a sense of belonging.

Yet for all this global perspective and transitoriness, people crave a sense of belonging. British people still have a preference for small intimate groups of friends rather than making new friends every five minutes. Thus churches with small groups may prosper and those groups may take priority over attending the amorphous congregational meeting on a Sunday. Such groups may be better suited to 'third place' environments rather than homes, especially for those whose jobs require them to live in another town a good deal of the time.

The title of Mark Knopfler's song, 'I need a little water of love', reminds us that people need more than material satisfaction, and who can miss the irony of Madonna's 'Material Girl'? God has set eternity in our hearts and we are restless until we find our rest in him. The search for human love is part of this yearning. People long for intimacy, trust and honesty. They long to feel appreciated and this even more so in a world that reduces us to a few manipulable digits for the convenience of faceless commercial and governmental interests. Who really knows us any more?

To meet this need, people resort to a great variety of social engagements – anything from evening classes to blind date meetings in pubs and clubs, from lingerie parties to theatre groups, from sports clubs to wine-tasting sessions. We yearn to belong, and the party – any kind of party – is where we find that possibility.

The church has a powerful role to play in this once it gets beyond its obsession with bums on seats on a Sunday morning and begins to contextualise the faith in people's real life needs and to take a genuine interest in their well-being. The churches that are doing this are also growing.

There are other casualties of change but I selected these three because they reflect the sense of alienation felt by many in our society, and alienation invites reconciliation. Far from being discouraged, we need to see that such a world is gospel territory. Our reconciled lives and our sense of belonging to one another in community, once divested of its ghettoism, is a powerful medicine for the ills of our society.

So, what now?

- Does the loss of Christian tradition in our society make you angry, sad, discouraged and defensive or optimistic, challenged and inventive? What will you do with these emotions?
- Do you prefer your theology as a list of propositions or as a dynamic experience of God in your life situation? Or is it a combination of the two?
- How many casualties of change does your church serve each week? Which practical programmes address which needs?

8
Cyborgs for Jesus

Technology drives change, making possible the seemingly impossible and extending human capabilities far beyond anything our forefathers might have dreamed. With so many machines to relieve the drudgery of life, we are free to extend our boundaries and our personalities.

Treble double you dot com

Once upon a time I had an identity defined by the culture in which I was raised. Not any more. Like Madonna I may assume any number of serial identities and, with the help of the Internet, why not all at once? Today's web wizard can create as many URLs as he wishes and adopt different personas for each. He might run a football club news site, be part of a popular medical advice panel for blokes, participate in a voyeur's chat room, run a vintage car magazine trading company, and be in dating correspondence with an oriental girl he has never met. Indeed, since no one need ever meet you, how do they know which, if any, is the real you? Or is the real you, in fact, this composite treble double you – a mosaic persona for a mosaic culture?

Monoculture churches are in trouble at this point. All those who aim to be the ideal church will have to ask themselves the question, 'Ideal for whom?' If the church is to have a future in this mission field, it must cease to treat its own particular culture as a tenet of faith. We need a diverse range of expressions of what it means to be the body of Christ, and none of them must claim superiority over another. Since so much of our disunity, criticism, suspicion and competitiveness has to do with cultural and traditional preferences this may be a great opportunity to repent of these vices by learning to respect diversity as a God-given blessing. The leaders of the future will embrace multiculturalism with open arms.

Does this mean that life will become so individualised that any form of corporate belief is impossible? Does the shift from 'one size fits all' to 'tailor made' rule out the possibility of the worshipping community? Far from it; the desire for individual identity carries with it the search for others of similar identities. We want to belong, but with people like ourselves. Hassle-free relationships for people on the move. So networking is big, special interest groups are in and parties are where we meet people of our kind. We wear our subtle badges – body piercing, tattoos, shaved heads, make-up, fashion wear, designer labels, shades, accessories – to indicate our type to others and to make those connections that give us a sense of clannish and even tribal identity.

If the church is to make any impact in the future then it must find ways of combining its ideal of 'all one in Christ Jesus' with the reality of very distinct cultural groupings, without favouring any one of them above the other. The future will belong to those who know how to network these cultural groups into an organic whole using the services of connectors, specialists and salespeople – pastors, teachers and evangelists – rather than those who try to impose a monoculture from the pulpit.

Techno-spirituality

Gary is a neo-pagan. No, he is not a dark demon worshipper. His ritual sacrifices are offered to influence cosmic energies rather than to please the gods. Gary isn't religious, but he is spiritual; he believes that life is full of mysteries that cannot be satisfactorily answered by appeals to a transcendent God, nor by science alone. The world is about energy; there is a mystical connection between the material and Mater, the Earth Mother upon whom we all depend, and Gary wants to explore it.

His journey has taken him down many esoteric paths: he has tried to develop Gaia sensitivity, he has attended positive visualisation courses, has experimented with Tantric sex, joined pilgrimages to ancient sites of spirituality, created a feng shui business environment, tried amulets, meditation crystals, statuettes, sexual fetishes, essential oils, learned mantras, spells and astrology, sat at the feet of a Druidic guru, joined every new age network he could find, experienced astral travel – anything, any spiritual technology that might help him tap into the cosmic force to his advantage.

> We will not bring Gary to faith in Christ by waving placards outside the local occult fair. We might do better by taking a stall inside.

We will not bring Gary to faith in Christ by waving placards outside the local occult fair. We might do better, as some

Christians have done, by taking a stall inside the fair and offering to help people in their search for spiritual reality. Recently, in an inner-city market, believers have been offering fortune cookies from an old Brethren promise box (Scripture text lucky dip) to passers-by and then offering to pray the scripture into the recipient's life. It has led to many fruitful conversations. In one US city local Christians offer dream interpretation in the local secular bookstore. The uptake is amazing and leads to serious opportunities for faith sharing.

Gary won't be reached by conventional religion but his hunger and curiosity for all things spiritual and esoteric provides an open door for those who are prepared to lead him to 'know the mystery of God, namely, Christ, in whom are hidden all the treasures of wisdom and knowledge' (Colossians 2:3). Paul borrowed the proto-Gnostic language of the mystery cults to present Christ as the true goal of the spiritual journey. Maybe we should be less precious about some of our language. In my book about the Harry Potter phenomenon I suggested as a way for reaching the Garys of this world that the

> old religion is not old enough, for, 'In the beginning was the Spell, and the Spell was with God, and the Spell was God . . . and the Spell became human and lived among us, full of grace and truth.' The ultimate effectual word – that is what a spell claims to be – is a Person, the Logos, the Son of God who on the cross, in C.S. Lewis' words, performed a 'deeper magic' that disspells evil and opens the path of transformational enlightenment through spiritual union with himself. (Those who object to my use of Spell to translate Logos might prefer Empowered Seminal Reason, but I am trying to reach twenty-first-century pagans not

first-century pagans. Word, in our current use of the term, is an inadequate translation.)[1]

And why not describe yourself as a spiritual healer? You can always say that your spiritual Master is Jesus, and maybe especially if the person is healed get the chance to explain what is unique about Jesus and why he died and rose again. And why should I not use the Hindu word 'guru' to describe myself if I am reaching Hindus, rather than the Latin word 'pastor'?

Consumed with desire

In 1988 I wrote a spoof advertisement to illustrate for a group of would-be writers the power of imagination. It was for a fast motor car and it went something like this: '*The untamed panther is at your command. Unleash the beast and ride like the wind! Sheer throbbing power. Smooth muscular strength devouring the miles. Crouch into the bends and sense the snarling force run through your spine. For you, the car, the animal spirit, are one!*' All it needs is footage of a panther on the loose coming to a panting halt before a cool, sexy lady – and one shot of the car in the background.

Sadly, I never tried to sell the concept, but within a few years the style had become commonplace. No longer do we point out the technical or comfort aspects of a vehicle. Now our sales pitch promises personal enhancement, emotional satisfaction and most often sexual success. For to be sellable you have to be sexy.

We are a generation of consumers. Conservation may be

---

[1] *A Closer Look at Harry Potter* (Kingsway 2001).

politically correct but we consume as never before. Our lives really do consist in the abundance of our possessions. This consumer mentality is all-pervasive and is set to be the dominant feature in our early twenty-first-century lives. It even enters our intimate relationships; for many sex has become a consumer item, a recreation for the moment with whomever we please for our immediate gratification, rather than an act that reflects a covenant of mutual giving. For the point of consumerism is personal satisfaction in exchange for money, not the selling of ourselves. Indeed we consumers are very protective of ourselves. Not only do we want guarantees that safeguard us from fraudulent products and sellers but we want to know that the product will gratify us without changing us. It must fit me; I don't alter to fit it. It must give to me; beyond the asking price, I do not expect to give of myself.

Some have sold out and have marketed their church to be just another product on the cultural shelves meeting all the felt needs of the consumers.

It affects our perception of church. More and more church leaders complain that they are serving a consumer market rather than people who are there to learn how to be better servants of the Master. Some have sold out and have marketed their church to be just another product on the cultural shelves meeting all the felt needs of the consumers. The price may be the heart of the gospel. Jesus said, 'If anyone would come after me, he must deny himself and take up his cross and follow me. For whoever wants to save his life will lose it, but whoever loses his life for me will find it' (Matthew 16:24–25). Hardly a good selling point! Nor can the crucifixion by any stretch of sane imagination be classed as sexy.

However, Michael Moynagh makes the telling point that the problem is not so much what we should be saying but where we are saying it. The leisure environment demands entertainment, pleasure, gratification, but the work environment, although nowadays needing to become much more fulfilling, can only function on the basis of truth, values, quality and trust. Guess where the church should be proclaiming its message! Frankly, we are in the wrong place for our sort of message and our kind of communication. We are disconnected from the one environment where we could be heard with a degree of objectivity and we are trying to be objective in the one environment where it is almost impossible to be heard. A major rethink on the location of the church and the 'pulpit' seems in order.

The majority of Christians are as much part of this consumer society as the non-Christians. If you want to lead a twenty-first-century church God's way then you will have to offer something more radical than self-indulgence in religious gift wrap, but you will have to do so in the world where people spend the majority of their waking hours.

Engineered for life

The twenty-first century will be the bionomic century in which we will become used to the fusion of organic and non-organic materials to create remarkable new products and computers that make our current ones look as slow as an abacus. The nuclear age has given way to the age of the nucleus. Genetic engineering is the technology of tomorrow and it will profoundly affect all our lives. Some breakthroughs are really good. My wife is diabetic and like millions of others benefits from genetically engineered human insulin that is so much more compatible than the stuff that was formerly extracted from slaughtered animals.

Other matters are of greater concern. People rightly fear the impact of GM foods being foisted on the planet by unscrupulous multinational agrochemical companies who do not know the long-term effects of their products on either the environment or the consumers.

The other spectacle is that of human cloning and the development of human stem cell technology using fertilised human ova. As I write, in spite of all the moral objections, a group have claimed that they are already producing cloned human beings. Like it or not, if a technology is possible then it will be used somewhere and almost certainly for military purposes. There is no going back to yesterday's innocence where we only had to contend with weapons of nuclear mass destruction! Tomorrow may see a new breed of humans engineered to resist biological and chemical attacks. Yesterday's science fiction will become today's off-the-shelf product. With promises to cure all our ills, little is going to halt this juggernaut apart from either a dreadful catastrophe – or just maybe a return to ethically based theistic science that respects human life as made in the image of God. Church leaders today must learn how to apply the principles of an ancient book written in an agrarian society to what goes on in hi-tech labs on the university campus.

It will not be easy. If we want to defend the sanctity of human life we will have to contend not only with the issue of abortion but with the therapeutic offer of cloned embryo tissue as a means of curing children of inherited and other diseases. How will we advise parents? Will the church be the only place left where children are deformed because the parents refused to have them aborted, or refused the alternative of a healthily engineered implanted embryo? What kinds of pressure will this put on parents as the skills for caring for handicapped children are lost simply because most people opt not to let them be born in the first place? Will the children of my grandchildren be the only ones not engineered against biological weapons because their Christian values objected to cloned embryo tissue being injected into them?

> Soon the call to worship will come via your mobile phone and the sermon really will be a text message.

Or will the church gain great respect as, to use Richard Foster's words, 'a community of loving defiance' that is prepared to speak up for the poor and maimed and disadvantaged? If so, it must grapple with these issues not as part of a conservative right wing agenda but as a matter of well-considered principle that seeks to do all it can to uphold the dignity of the individual and to provide as much ethically acceptable remedial care as it possibly can.

There is no going back on technology. The hands that are raised in worship tomorrow may well have microchips embedded into them enabling the offering to be electronically transferred by the simple laying on of hands! Cyberspace church is already emerging and soon the call to worship will come via your mobile phone and the sermon really will be a text message. Nor need this be restricted to one country; the church of the future really can be universal in scope, with all of us connected all of the time. Never will the integrity of the message have been more important.

So, what now?

- Identify the people groups in your church. Do your services satisfy everyone or are some parts an endurance test for some people groups? In what contexts do you find everyone is happy?
- How do you respond to new age spirituality? Are you uncritical of it or do you view it as satanic? Try describing your own spirituality in new age terms.
- What matters most to you: information or inspiration? Imagine combining both in a workplace or campus-based church.

9
Tell Us a Story

Recently we attended a relative's wedding and were struck by the unbelievable number of photographs and video clips being taken. There were so many cameo pieces that it seemed like a photo shoot for Weddings on a Simply Enormous Budget Magazine. What, we asked, did we do before the invention of the camera?

We told stories, that's what – and then we embellished them. 'Auntie Sue stumbling into a male guest on a step' after thirty years became 'Auntie Sue blind drunk and trying to get off with every man in sight'. And, man, what we did to the car! Gossip is the stuff of legends, and so much more interesting than mere photographs.

We humans love our myths and every age has them. In the past, myths evolved from human experience, from the eccentricities, adventures and failings of men. They involved real families, dynasties and heroic deeds of war and exploration. The national gods had their part to play too.

The new myths

All that has changed. Today, myths are commercially manu-
factured for an international market involving vast sums of
money and they find their way into our lives through films,
DVDs and books – and mostly in that order. Even the traditional myths, like Robin Hood, are ripped from their cultural
context and repackaged for global consumption.

These movie myths are increasingly about special effects,
fantastical settings and stylised characters. As such they have
entertainment value but seldom produce the reflectivity of the
older myths. There are exceptions. *Indecent Proposal*, for
instance, had many people asking the relevant question,
'What price do you put on love and sexual fidelity?', and *The
Matrix* invited us to explore the degree to which we have
become state-controlled machines. Even the feel-good film *My
Big, Fat Greek Wedding* prompted us to reflect on the loss of
relational fulfilment found among many middle-class Anglo-
Saxons, while underneath the blood and thunder of the film
version of *The Lord of the Rings* lie many lessons about the
values that matter to us in times of crisis.

The lesser narrative cousin to the movie is television, and in
particular the soaps watched by millions on a daily basis and
into which are woven not only the lives of the characters but
the changing values of our society. Soaps provide us with a
reflective medium for considering the ethical implications of
our actions on our relationships with others – a factor too
often discounted by academics and preachers alike, who tend
to concentrate much more on the principles at stake. Guess
who gets the bigger audience.

Nor is the book dead. In fact it is thriving as never before, with Great Britain alone publishing some 90,000 new titles a year, many of them fiction. Much of it is, like television and film, sheer escapism to help us while away the hours on the aeroplane or to complement the tanning process on the beach; but many books compel us to think about life. For example, I know of no better exposition of the issues surrounding the death penalty than *The Chamber* by John Grisham, and although we may currently be selling our souls to the devil on this one, the term 'big brother' has entered the language from George Orwell's *1984* and it still exercises the power of caution in many of our minds.

In this age of multitudinous stories, the Christian tale has some pretty heavy competition. We fight for air time; we struggle to tell it well; we fear to add or subtract to the Scriptures in the process. Yet one thing is certain: whoever has the most persuasive story to tell will win the day, and that is profoundly important for us all.

The medium owns the message

'What is truth?' Pilate asked Jesus. The answer today is simple: whatever the media want it to be. The recent success of *Big Brother*, a fly-on-the-wall serial where a bunch of people are locked away in an artificial house and are videoed twenty-four hours a day, illustrates the point. To make the 'real life' programme work, the producers find people who are anything but normal and who inevitably play their part well for the cameras. The footage is edited to make good television – it has to concentrate on the eccentricities and outrages, the emotional highlights and the relational tensions between the competing participants. People then vote for their favourites according to what the producers have predisposed them to vote.

Live TV isn't. Pictures and words can all be digitalised, manipulated and seamlessly re-presented in a form quite unlike the original. Indeed, an original is no longer necessary.

To make the 'real life' programme work, the producers find people who are anything but normal.

The power of producers is awesome and film stars will have to copyright and licence their binary profile, necessitating a whole new set of laws about how much computer code comprises the essence of an actor. Perhaps none of this would pose a problem if those concerned were people of high moral integrity and were driven by a commitment to the truth. That is seldom the case; people are driven by other agendas and often this means that truth is what they want it to be. Sadly, this is especially true of our news media, where outrages against 'politically incorrect' groups such as Christians are routinely either not reported or misreported.

In a world where objectivity is strongly subjected to entertainment value, there is a real difficulty for truth-focused believers in getting a hearing either inside or outside the media without sounding boring and therefore being unacceptable. What then of the earnest preacher using no more props than a pair of hands?

If we wish to impact our twenty-first-century culture, we will need to catch up on our communications skills and on our technology and styles of presentation. This is much more than whether or not we install data projectors in our sanctuaries. I can see little point in such technology if we are only projecting the words of our songs and the points of the preacher's monologue. The OHP will do just as well. The deeper questions remain about where we teach, who teaches, what constitutes the most suitable format for teaching, and how we create cybernetic loops that continue the process beyond the last hymn.

The divine drama

Revelation is mediated through redemptive experience. The Bible is a divinely attested drama – the unfolding adventures of God and his people, and the progressive self-revelation of God's nature. Truth is never abstract but is rooted in particular history. The Ten Commandments were given at a particular time to a people who needed a standard of conduct that would enable them to live together in the most extreme conditions. That these laws, in the purpose of God, prove to have universal validity is consequent upon the special experience of a horde of Hebrew refugees rather than an academy of theology and ethics. The great doctrine of justification by faith owes its origin to a stargazer named Abraham, who believed God and it was accounted to him as righteousness (Genesis 15:5–6). All Paul's exposition of this truth goes back to the historical experience of a wealthy but childless nomad.

This divine drama reaches its climax not in the doctrine of the Person of Christ but in the advent of Jesus into the world at a particular time and place in history. He is a first-century Jewish male artisan, and his mum's name is Mary. Those who are open to the revelation will discover through the record of his life that he is also the Christ, the Son of the living God.

This narrative approach to theology does not come naturally

to many who, like myself, were taught systematic, analytical theology at both Bible college and church. We will have to pass through the painful experience of feeling unsound, superficial and illogical if we are to discover how to bring truth to this generation. It is essential that we do if we want to equip our people for mission. Rather than declaiming, in good old Billy Graham fashion, 'The Bible says . . .' we need an approach that begins 'Do you know the story of . . .?' or 'Have you heard the one about . . .?' Nor, with care, will a little imagination go amiss. I occasionally do the one about the Woman of Some Area, a

We will have to pass through the painful experience of feeling unsound, superficial and illogical.

buxom barmaid with whom Jesus had a conversation when he dropped in for a lunchtime pint while his disciples went off in the Ford Transit to get some grub from Burger King. It allows me to make all the usual points about spiritual discernment, divorce and remarriage, the problems with religion and the new age that Jesus introduced, but in a way that captures the imagination. They are contemporary issues, after all . . .

The privatisation of faith

One of the most significant features of early twenty-first-century life in Britain is the privatisation of faith and belief. True, you can believe what you like, but you mustn't talk about it. Censorious legislation, political correctness and social conformity make it uncool and unacceptable to declare your faith, let alone attempt proselytising. This especially applies to those in positions of power such as school teachers or managers, but it has extended to all areas of public and work life. We also suffer from extensive media censorship and religious discrimination against evangelical Christianity in this country, forcing us into the unwelcome position of a marginalised and intellectually persecuted minority group. Thankfully, there are many who stand against this intolerance but they have to work extraordinarily hard to find an acceptable opportunity to share their faith.

One of the consequences of religious privatisation is the loss of religious language, a phenomenon more pronounced among men than women. The latter seem to have retained a language of spirituality and most women's magazines devote space to a variety of new age topics. This is less so among men. A great missiological challenge facing the church is the need to create a language of faith that can be used by blokes. Unless we address this we shall be unable to communicate the gospel to 80 per cent of the men in our nation.

This privatisation of faith is the result of an intolerant tolerance. It is the will of both our UK and our European governments that we should tolerate all belief systems provided they do not manipulate or coerce their followers. In their idealised world we would have one pluralistic religion in which all the major systems had a part to play. Thus, it is believed, would end the obscenities of Northern Ireland, the Balkans and the Middle East alike.

Postmodernism tries to avoid judgementalism. Your belief is OK; mine is OK too. In part this is welcome, not least because we can charge those who criticise our faith as being politically incorrect and out of touch with where society is, and we can claim our right to a fair pitch in the market-place of ideas. But it is not all plain sailing, for Christianity is an exclusive religion on three main counts:

- It is the only one that offers a personal relationship with God.
- Jesus is the Son of God and the only way of salvation.
- Obedience to Christ requires us to evangelise every person on earth.

The powers that be know this and are cautious about giving us too much space. In practice they give us very little and their tolerance proves to be intolerant of our perceived intolerance. However hard we try to be nice – and we should try – we must face the fact that the gospel is still a stumbling block to the religious and madness to the intelligentsia; it carries its own built-in offence. We may call for a radical rethink of church and a re-examination of our beliefs and how we communicate them in the light of the mission field around us, but that is not to say the church must become a chameleon, constantly changing colour to blend into the background. There is a price to be paid for standing up for truth and justice, and there remain points where we must obey God rather than men.

So, what now?

- The Bible is mostly a collection of true stories. Why have we reduced them to a set of doctrinal statements and academic discussions?
- Rehearse your own story of God's grace. Try writing it down or sharing it with friends. Do so without quoting proof texts or using theological jargon.
- How do we draw the line between the offence of the gospel and presenting it in an offensive manner? What guidelines would you offer?

10
The Transforming Presence

Whether people attend church or not, and I use that term to cover the whole raft of programmes that we put on, will be determined by the needs and aspirations of their culture, not of ours, and unless we are prepared to engage with that culture and address those needs in the contemporary idiom, we shall remain a fringe ghetto movement.

Once we make the paradigm shift from *in here/out there* to *out here/in there*, from the centrality of the gathered model to the centrality of the diffused model, we must ask ourselves some profound questions about the nature of such a church and what it means to be a member of it. Defining the old paradigm is relatively easy because we have enough examples to copy. Yet the old model consists of literally hundreds of divisions over style, form and membership. Is the sacrament of bread and wine central, or the sacrament of the word, or the sacrament of the time of worship? Do you join through infant baptism or adult baptism or neither? Is the government episcopal or congregational or presbyterian? And that's only the start!

new paradigm of church simplifies all this because it focuses on values, qualities of life and relationship rather than regulations, traditions and historic divisions. Its emphasis is on the life out here rather than the conduct of club meetings.

Incarnational missionary communities

I like to describe the local manifestations of new-paradigm church as incarnational missionary communities. I do not use 'congregations' because that still leaves us in the old-paradigm thinking, which focuses on buildings and meetings rather than the life of Christ outworked in the community.

What does it mean to be part of an incarnational missionary community called church? When God wanted to say 'I love you', he turned up in person. The incarnation of Christ is the central theme of our faith. Long hinted at in the Old Testament through those fascinating and somewhat ambiguous incarnational appearances of the Lord or the Angel of the Lord, the coming of Christ split history down the middle. Until that time the word was on scrolls and in the mouths of prophets. Now the Word was on two legs; it had become enfleshed. Until that point the word was the law of Moses. Now the Word was grace and truth.

When God wanted to say 'I love you', he turned up in person. Jesus was no mere prophet or substitute for God. He wasn't a second-hand mouthpiece but the personal revelation of God himself: 'Anyone who has seen me has seen the Father' (John 14:9). We need no persuading that God is a Personality once we have met Jesus! Nor need we doubt that he wishes to

relate to us. All this has profound implications for how we ~~do~~
mission.

Gone are the days when we can hope to reach our society
by opening the doors of our buildings on Sundays and
hoping they will come flooding in. Nor will television and
radio effectively reach the majority in the West. People are
too dedicated to the programmes of their choice and there is
no compelling reason why the majority should tune in to a
Christian station. These may serve the Christian audience
but they will scarcely touch the non-Christian. Tracts
through the letter-box will go the way of all junk mail.
Shouting at people from street corners will do no more than
make them quicken their pace or cross the road. Knocking
on doors is a positive threat in days when people fear strang-
ers on the doorstep. The only effective way to present
church to the world is to be there at the personal level, to
incarnate something of Christ through the medium of our
own presence.

It demands of us that we prioritise the importance of relationship above structures and programmes. This is surprisingly radical.

Relational, creational, transformational

The people of the New Jerusalem have compromised with
the Harlot of Babylon. We have done so not by committing
some terrible sexual sin but whenever we have put the creational before the relational. In Romans 1:25, Paul indicts the
world with this charge, 'They . . . worshipped and served
created things rather than the Creator.' This simple statement is not merely addressing the creation v. evolution

debate but touches every aspect of human society. We must content ourselves with just two illustrations of what this means – one from everyday life and one from church life.

Education today is curriculum driven and is determined by criteria laid down by the government. It takes place in a standardised environment with set hours and set standards for measuring the performance of both teachers and students. The latter are required to fit into this created framework, irrespective of their personalities, gifts and aspirations. Teachers are supposed to be dedicated detached professionals, communicating the syllabus without reference to their own character or history. Little surprise then that education fails most of its participants. How different it would be if we began with a set of interpersonal relationships that would determine the best mode of education for each child, so that, as C.S. Lewis memorably put it, education became propagation rather than just propaganda. By subsuming the relational to the created we fail to make education a transformational experience.

How many a Sunday school teacher has done the job for half a lifetime simply because they were the only volunteer at the time?

My second example concerns the programmatic nature of most churches. The average church is run on a predetermined pattern into which people are expected to fit as best they can – and that often includes the leaders, some of whom feel like square pegs in round holes. Sometimes those patterns are centuries old and attain the status of tradition. Yet since when did Jesus call us to fit someone else's pattern, especially in a different culture and a different age? The whole point of his words to the woman at the well is that worship is not to do with set places and rituals but with the attitude of the heart: 'God is spirit, and his worshippers must worship in spirit and in truth' (John 4:24).

Spirituality is too often assessed by our attendance at the right meetings, or by our willingness to use our leisure time to serve projects and programmes thought up by the leaders, even if we are quite unsuited to the task. How many a Sunday school teacher has done the job for half a lifetime simply because they were the only volunteer at the time? It might have been more fruitful if we had put on a children's programme that was born out of the relational desire of a group of individuals to serve those children.

Many church leaders are desperate to find a programme that will make their church bigger. We buy into other people's success stories, often set in quite different cultures from our own, and then impose the package on our people with as much rigour as we hold to the orthodoxy of our creeds. Some of these projects and ideas are very good, but so often we impose this creational package with scant attention to the relationships between our people. 'We are going to launch Alpha, cell church, seeker-friendly services, Willow Creek – and next week you will all find yourselves in new groups!' No wonder the anticipated transformation never really takes place.

This prioritising of the created thing over the relational is just as idolatrous in the church as it is in the world. It is time to repent, to change our minds. A truly Christian worldview radically revises the order. It is something we must grasp if we want to make a transforming impact on our world.

In a proper Christian worldview the relational has absolute priority over the creational. It is a half-truth to say that we must get back to the creation, as opposed to beginning with redemption; we must go back further, back before anything was made, when God the Father, Son and Holy Spirit dwelt in an eternal relationship of love. It was out of this relationship that God said, 'Let *us* make man in our image' (Genesis 1:26).

The cosmos is the way it is and not something else, because this is what the divine relationship would produce. There could be no other universe unless there were another kind of God; we are made the way we are because we image the unique relationship found within the Trinity. The created both reflects and serves that relationship.

A major part of God's plan to reconcile all things to himself lies in getting this order right. Imagine a society where every project, every operation, every development, every employment is birthed from the particular relationships of individuals who between them create a whole range of transformational synergies.

Applying this principle to church life will require us to examine all our traditions both distant and recent, all our programmes and plans, in the light of this priority of the relational. Instead of trying to fill gaps or to provide a full-orbed consumer-led programme run by volunteers, or organising people into groups to serve a predetermined plan, we will concentrate on developing sets of relationships and on releasing their creational energies for the benefit of the kingdom. This *may* mean that some people run with Alpha or cell, or whatever. It may well be that they will come up with

When Jesus comes to the blind man, he does not bring a healing technique. Instead, he engages the man as a person.

effective mission strategies that are quite unique to their situation. One thing is certain: they will not be clones!

Once we have the order correct we can be in faith for transformation to take place. God will do his 'immeasurably more' because we are putting the priority where he puts it.

Transformation is more than mere growth. It is miraculous change brought about by the intervention of another realm into our situation. It is the exponential leap into another level. When Jesus comes to the blind man, he does not bring a healing technique. Instead, he engages the man as a person: 'What do you want me to do for you?' Upon the man's relational, personal response of faith, 'Lord, that I may receive my sight,' Jesus acts. The result? A blind man does receive his sight. Transformation indeed!

This is why praying together is so important. As we seek to develop a relational communion between one another and God, so his creative will is released, but it is done so with a transformational power built in. What a difference between our ideas that we then ask God to bless – and bless he does to a modest measure – and those that are born from people praying together. Most of the great Third World breakthroughs in the gospel have come not from evangelistic programmes, particular doctrinal emphases or techniques, but from corporate prayer. Even here we are in danger in the West because we immediately assume that if we can organise people into prayer groups and endow those groups with names cloned from other nations, we will get the same results. If we want to see real transformation, we must begin with those who want to pray because God has laid it on their hearts. Even if that is a small number to begin with, there is more hope for success than with a programme of prayer imposed by centralised leadership.

Jesus direct

Probably the greatest abuse of power in the church is our mediating of the Mediator through our structures and programmes. Our creational priority hinders access to Jesus. Even our theology can do this, especially if we teach from an Enlightenment mind-set that systematises the Son of God and requires that before we can really know Jesus for ourselves we must grasp the doctrine of the Person of Christ and express that in culturally agreed forms. This was not how the disciples got to know him.

No Bible teacher if pressed would be able to support such an approach from Scripture, and yet in practice this is what we imply. Jesus can be found, yes – as we follow a particular form of worship, embrace a style of music, use acceptable body language, say the right words, demonstrate our obedience to him by attendance and performance. And this is meant to lead to loving intimacy!

I am not opposed to sound doctrine, nor to meetings and programmes. I am simply insisting that we introduce Jesus direct and let these other matters flow from that relationship. How sad that so many of our introductory courses concentrate on conveying words of information about the Christian life rather than introducing the Word of Life himself. It may appear simplistic, but when people really encounter the Lord, most of their other problems start to be solved. It takes relatively little instruction to provide the necessary guidance in particular matters, once the heart is submitted to him.

I write this, not as a man who despises learning, but as someone who has been a Bible teacher all his adult life. Yet I am struck again and again by the difference between our theological education, with its detachment from the personal, and that of the New Testament. That great theologian of the early church, the apostle Paul, had a remarkably simple gospel: 'I passed on to you as of first importance: that Christ died for our sins according to the Scriptures, that he was buried, that he was raised on the third day according to the Scriptures, and that he appeared . . .' (1 Corinthians 15:3–5). In another place he says, 'I resolved to know nothing while I was with you except Jesus Christ and him crucified' (1 Corinthians 2:2). The clue lies in his passion for Jesus direct: 'I want to know Christ . . .' (Philippians 3:10).

Once we really grasp this principle of direct relationship with Christ we will be much better able to affirm people on their journey towards Christ. I recently met an older man who had been a Christian for all of his conscious life and yet who felt he had no real testimony because he could not name the day and the hour when he prayed the sinner's prayer! God help us. This man knew Jesus; he had crossed many bridges in life in the company of Jesus; he had a fine story to tell of Christ in all aspects of his life. Yet because in his church background Jesus was mediated through a formula, he felt spiritually second class. It should never have been so.

Jesus is the one mediator between God and man (1 Timothy 2:5). We should not let ourselves or our programmes, or our doctrinal structures, or our ecclesiastic preferences become a mediator between us and him.

Jesus direct also reminds us that God did not send an angel but came himself in real flesh and blood. The mission mandate of the church, likewise, cannot be fulfilled by remote control. The incarnation has changed history; from now on the Word must always be made flesh – and we are that flesh, if we truly constitute the body of Christ. Videos, tracts and broadcasts all have their role but never as a substitute for personal relationships. Christianity is caught not taught; it really is propagation rather than propaganda. If we want to introduce people to Jesus then we must be Jesus towards them. This is why we must engage prophetically with the community and with the culture. As he is in the world, so are we – sharing its joys and sorrows, speaking its language, ministering to its needs, challenging its falsehoods and redeeming its people.

The more effective we become at this, the less we will find ourselves relying on learned techniques and formulae; the Jesus we invite folk to commit their lives to will be no freshly introduced stranger, but the Jesus they have already encountered through the impact of our lives.

I try to approach life like this: my pilgrimage touches all sorts of other people on their own pilgrimages. For whatever length of time I walk with them, be it sometimes ever so brief, I want something of Jesus himself to touch them and to help them take one step closer to him. It may be a modest aspiration, but it's real; it's Jesus as direct as I know how.

Less a religion, more a partnership

One of the often quoted characteristics of the early disciples, noted by their enemies, was that they had been with Jesus (Acts 4:13). It needs to become the chief attribute of God's people. Too often, in spite of our protests to the contrary, we lay ourselves open to the charge of being just another religion. That is because we are apt to behave religiously! Our ritualistic, stereotypical, structured patterns of speech and behaviour look to a postmodern world like the manifestations of psychologically repressed and fearful personalities, and everyone knows that religion is for emotional cripples!

Christianity should be the least religious of the religions. It is all to do with Christ: he in us and us in him. The life we live is his life lived out through our personalities. We are in a partnership with him. I prefer partnership in this context rather than the word 'relationship' simply because our union with Christ leads inevitably to creative and redemptive action. The partnership means that we are co-workers with him (2 Corinthians 6:1). How liberating that is! We have only to do what he is doing in active communion with him as well as with our fellow believers. Since Christ dwells in all our hearts by faith in ways that are unique for each one of us, we should actually be able to do what we are good at rather than simply fulfil the imposed expectations of others.

The most important thing about your life and mine is the transforming presence of Christ working in and through us by the Holy Spirit to fulfil the Father's will twenty-four hours a day, seven days a week, wherever we are. It is the starting point for church and the starting point for ministry.

So, what now?

- How well would your church function if it never met on a Sunday? Would it still be a supportive witnessing community?

- Examine your family, work and church life. Does the relational determine the creational, or is it the other way round? Take steps to remedy what you can.
- Imagine instead of a 'What would Jesus do?' wristband, you wore a 'What is Jesus doing?' one. Practise that new awareness in your own life.

11
Your Full-time Ministry

Incarnating Christ, working in partnership with him, is not restricted to so-called church activities. That is by far the smaller part of life, though you would scarcely believe it to talk with some leaders who think that their programmes and plans should have priority over everything else. It leads the gullible to despise their jobs as a necessary evil so that they can in their free time get on with 'the real work'. Folks, the real work of the Lord begins when you wake up and ends when you go to sleep, and even your sleep is part of that work. Every Christian is full time for Jesus and should be engaged in the mission of Christ. It is a privilege and an honour that isn't intended to exhaust us but to inspire us. Jesus' yoke is easy and his burden is light; anything more is a self-imposed handicap.

Every-member chaplaincy

I call this priestly role every-member chaplaincy; all of us are called to be chaplains in our homes, our workplaces and our communities. Now, before all the alarm bells sound off, this is not an attack on the professional priesthood; instead it represents a releasing of the full ministry of the body of Christ.

What is the task of a chaplain? He or she is placed in the environment to minister Christ's grace to the needs of others in a manner that is both relational and holistic. It does not mean that everyone is called to be an aggressive, scalp-hunting evangelist or to take a portable communion service when they catch the 0815! The majority of this chaplaincy work is fulfilled in the manner that we conduct our ordinary affairs, in the demeanour with which we handle our workaday life, in the grace we demonstrate when coping with people and problems, in the fact that our presence in the room brings an intangible but nevertheless real presence of Jesus. Our lives then become a sacrament and a sign of hope to all who wish to partake.

It means that our words and our works convey grace; the products of our labours are touched with the love of God. And, yes, because we take a genuine and prayerful interest in the holistic well-being of those around us, feeling pastorally responsible for our neighbours, we find appropriate opportunities to speak directly about our faith without the cringe factor kicking in.

It does not mean that everyone is called to be an aggressive, scalp-hunting evangelist or to take a portable communion service when they catch the 0815!

The people we serve in our homes may be children or unbelieving relatives. They may be friends to whom we show hospitality. In the workplace they are our colleagues, customers and creditors. In the community they are our neighbours, the people we meet up with at the sports club, pub or evening class. Few of them will formally ask us to be their chaplain; all of them need our ministry.

We can give this ministry a specific content framework by means of what I call the spirituality spiral, as in the diagram below. A significant aspect of the work of leadership in the new paradigm will be to ensure that God's people are thoroughly equipped in these five areas of life, not simply because we hope they will become good Christians but because every member of the church is now part of the work-force that leaders are responsible to send forth and to manage in the field of life.

The spirituality spiral

I have drawn this as a two-way spiral because the centre might just as well lead to the edge as the edge may lead to the centre. In other words, intimacy with God will lead us to form good relationships, but good relationships may also lead people to God.

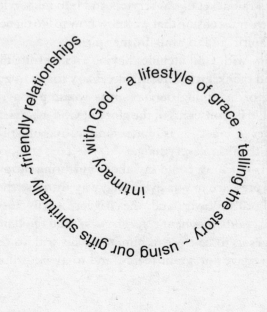

Intimacy with God

Every-member chaplaincy means that we bring the intimate presence of God into people's lives. To do so we must ensure that our own relationship with God is sound. Good disciples of Jesus give attention to their devotional life not only in terms of particular activities such as prayer and Bible reading but also in cultivating their daily walk with God.

Many postmoderns, especially those of a new age disposition, are looking for a spiritual aura or emanation from those who claim spirituality. They are right to do so, though they often look for it in the wrong direction. Jesus was full of grace and truth; he radiated the presence of the Holy Spirit through every fibre of his being and without a trace of self-consciousness or otherworldly piety. We must do likewise and that means releasing the charismatic experience of the Holy Spirit from the religious straitjacket of our services and into the service of life. Our leaders must ensure that we know how to 'go on being filled with the Spirit' and to 'walk by the Spirit'.

Intimacy with God includes having an inner life filled with praise and thanksgiving. It isn't necessary for us to go around whistling or humming our favourite worship song, but our lives should be conscious of the glory of God wherever we are. The power of inner joy is immeasurable, and one of the keys is to give thanks in everything.

There is much we could say about nurturing the awareness of God's presence in our lives. One way is to use the stanzas of the Lord's Prayer and the trigger words '*belonging*', '*purpose*', '*empowerment*', '*forgiveness*' and '*guidance*'. This encourages us to be close to him, to do his will, to receive his help, to receive and grant mercy, and to avoid evil in favour of goodness. It's easy to remember and easy to do wherever we are.[1]

A lifestyle of grace

Every-member chaplaincy is a call to exercise a lifestyle of grace. This means not bowing to secular pressure on major issues or bowing to religious pressure on minor issues. Christianity properly lived is challenging, but it is also attractive. If we appear worse off because of our beliefs, we can hardly blame people if they don't want to buy the product. I am convinced that Jesus was the most attractive man who ever lived, both in his face, which was unmarred by lust, greed, arrogance or deceit, and in his winsome loving personality. Little wonder people followed this 'friend of sinners' who walked where they walked but without evil, and who demonstrated so dramatically the difference between heart obedience and external religious rigidity.

Grace does not compromise, but it is flexible, transcending the hard-line binary equations of religion that want every issue neatly answered yes or no, with appropriate rewards and punishments. The prophet Micah captured God's triad of grace perfectly: 'What does the Lord require of you? To act justly and to love mercy and to walk humbly with your God' (Micah 6:8). Holding those three principles in holy balance is the secret of living by grace. It will earn us respect for our high standards, for our compassionate application of those standards

> Grace, painfully clung to in the mystery of suffering, carries more appeal than magic-wand answers to prayer.

---

[1] I am indebted to John Twistleton for this way of looking at the prayer.

in the interests of others and for our humility in not claiming
to have all the answers. The impact of this approach is especially powerful in those situations, so common in human
experience, where we require some form of arbitration. Grace-
filled Christians make excellent mediators.

Telling the story

Every-member chaplaincy means that we each have a story to
tell. This doesn't mean we have to tell the whole story every
time we open our mouths! What we do have to share is our
ongoing experience of Christ. Every Christian needs to know
how to tell their own story without embarrassment, jargon
or hypocrisy. Just don't call it a testimony or a witness!
Significant as our crisis conversion might be, if we had one, it
is only a small part of the tale. Often what people need to hear
is just one small personal anecdote that captures our experience of Christ. It need not be a success story; grace, painfully
clung to in the mystery of suffering, carries more appeal than
magic-wand answers to prayer.

We need to be equipped to tell the story of Jesus in plain
non-technical language. In our desire for theological sound-
ness we neglect the gospel stories at our peril. Learn to narrate
them as though you were speaking to children. It hardly ever
fails! Jesus used stories, parables of grace, because he knew
that spiritual truth communicates not by proposition but by
metaphor; the story expresses the reality in such a way as to
lead us into an authentic spiritual encounter.

People are less willing to accept dogmatic, systematic asser-
tions about God or human behaviour. A postmodern generation will not buy God as a set of propositions, but they will
learn from stories. The significance of soaps as the most

popular form of television lies in the way they define world-views, and in the use of story as a vehicle for communicating particular moral and spiritual values.

Preachers have too often taught propositional theology from the pulpit in the way they learned it at Bible college and from books. Little wonder Christians find it hard to articulate their faith in the real world! The Bible is God's soap opera, a divine drama of epic proportions that communicates truth through the power of imagination. Jesus comes across as a real person in human history, supremely relevant to our lives today. Instead of debating unintelligible theological asser-tions, tell God stories. Better the parable of the Prodigal Son than to say, 'God will effect judicial and filial reconciliation with you if you penitentially acknowledge your spiritual bankruptcy and repent of all your lusts!'

Using our gifts spiritually

The fourth element in the spirituality spiral concerns using our gifts spiritually. I find it artificial to separate spiritual gifts from natural gifts, since both come from God. We should use all the gifts as the tools of grace with which to serve others in the course of life.

It is a grave disservice to the world to restrict the gifts to our meeting environments. For example, the world is crying out for prophecy; this is why so many people read their horoscopes and why the dubious prophecies of Nostradamus remain best-selling reading matter. How about us bringing true words of prophecy to our colleagues at work? What about asking God for a word of wisdom to release a problem in business? Why not offer to pray for a neighbour's stiff neck? The possibilities are endless. The person who takes a meal to an overworked mum with a sickly child, and does so consciously in the name of Jesus, is using her gift to serve the purposes of God. Who knows what transformational possibilities might arise from such acts of mercy?

Many people in our churches have an unnecessarily low image of themselves because they feel that their gifts are of no great value to the Lord. I have met head teachers, doctors, craftsmen, senior executives – some of the most talented people in our society – who consider that they have nothing to offer. It is because leaders make much only of their skills or those that are useful for leading meetings instead of affirming all God's people in their daily gifting.

Friendly relationships

The final aspect of every-member chaplaincy is the ability to be friendly. It is unrealistic to be close friends with everyone we meet, but as followers of Jesus we should be nice to know, easygoing, open hearted, cheerful, good to have around. People liked Jesus! Yet how often we enter the world domain like scared rabbits expecting at any moment to be devoured by a fox or run over by a truck! This is the Lord's earth and though it has many pitfalls for the foolish, we will find it a healthier place to live if we have the confidence that Christ is with us and his love is winning us a place in people's affections. Christianity, in the final analysis, is the art of friendly persuasion.

Some people find it easier than others to make friends; some can indulge in small talk till the cows come home, while others need a serious topic to get them started. But all of us are capable of a smile and a greeting – even if we have to practise it in front of the mirror! As a shy extrovert myself I prefer others to introduce me, but I have learned the art of getting people to talk about their favourite subject, which is usually themselves, and that prevents me from having to worry about my own performance.

Many Christians emit an aura of aloofness and judgementalism, not because they are arrogant (though some are) but because they are trying to be holy. Never try to be holy; it is painful to behold! Instead, relax into your security in Christ, politely refuse the things you know to be wrong and enjoy all the rest along with your colleagues. Once you relax, so will they and that opens the door for the grace of God far better than any defensive 'stand'.

Post-Bible Christianity

The Bible may still be the world's best-selling book but it is probably still one of the least read. In spite of all the sermons on the matter and the admirable efforts of the Bible societies and Bible reading fellowships, the majority of Western Christians do not read their Bibles either regularly or thoroughly.

I used to worry about this until I realised that no Christians in the early church read their Bibles. The reason was simple: they didn't have them. The Old Testament scriptures were jealously guarded in Jewish synagogues and only the wealthier congregations were likely to possess a full set. The New Testament had not yet been written in its full form and the most a congregation might possess was a copy of one of Paul's letters or maybe a Gospel. The majority had nothing. It wasn't

The two testaments bound in leather covers just didn't exist. Yet these people managed to change the world.

even a case of widespread illiteracy; the two testaments bound
in leather covers just didn't exist. Yet these people managed to
change the world.

They did so simply by being the Bible on two legs. Paul
states it thus: 'You are a letter from Christ, the result of our
ministry, written not with ink but with the Spirit of the living
God, not on tablets of stone but on tablets of human hearts'
(2 Corinthians 3:3). The secret of these early believers was
that they could live out and tell the story of Jesus and their
own transforming encounter with him. It proved sufficient to
change an empire.

I am not wishing to minimise the value of the Bible as we
have it today, nor do I wish to deny the importance of reading
it, or at least listening to it being read. Reading the Bible
played a significant part in my journey to Christ, but then I am
among those classed as highly literate and reading is a natural
way for me to gain information. This is not necessarily so in
our society where practical illiteracy, short-term concentration spans and the impact of the televisual medium mean that
the majority of our population are not likely to pick up a Bible
by choice. However, the Bible they will read is the one that
speaks and lives the truth in the form of a human being.

Our church leaders have a dual responsibility here. They
must ensure that people's lives are governed by the plumb-line
of truth as revealed in the Scriptures, rather than by a mere
consensus of subjective experiences. They must also train us
to interact with the text and context of the word so that it
becomes naturally our truth articulated in our normal language and idiom. The public lecturing that we call preaching
is not the best way to do this!

The only way that a truth can become my truth, the way the

gospel became for Paul, *my gospel*, is for me to engage with it. However much we may lack the preacher's fluency or understanding, we need to articulate the truth for ourselves, to discuss it, to argue it out, to challenge it with all the honest questions that our non-Christian friends might ask. This is one of those cybernetic loops: what we believe makes us what we are, and what we are reveals what we believe. The only truth that we ultimately understand and truly believe is the one that we have learned to live – and that is the truth that will most powerfully impact those around us.

So, what now?

- List your work colleagues, fellow students, immediate family and friends. This is your congregation. Consider how you can help them closer to Jesus.
- Check out the spirituality spiral in your own life. Imagine what impact you make on your daily acquaintances by putting yourself in their shoes.
- The truth you live is the only truth you understand. Write down three biblical truths that you wish to weave into your life.

12

Powerful Powerlessness

The new-paradigm churches are committed to holistic mission. Believing with the psalmist that the earth is the Lord's and everything in it, and that Jesus is the rightful heir of the nations, they are determined to bring his redemptive blessing to every sphere of human activity. No door is considered closed, no nation unreachable, no work too hard – or too unspiritual. Whatever your occupation, whatever task you perform, menial or mighty, it is an expression of worship and service for his kingdom. No one need ever again doubt that they have a ministry and a calling that is worthy of their Lord and Saviour.

We are the army of ordinary people, a grass-roots multitude with an extraordinary sense of shared mission. Our profile is low but it is as pervasive as salt and as persuasive as light.

Holy subversion

With the apostle Paul we recognise the essential futility and wilfulness of society without God: 'They are darkened in their understanding and separated from the life of God because of the ignorance that is in them due to the hardening of their hearts. Having lost all sensitivity, they have given themselves over to sensuality so as to indulge in every kind of impurity, with a continual lust for more' (Ephesians 4:18–19). In addition, 'The god of this age has blinded the minds of unbelievers, so that they cannot see the light of the gospel of the glory of Christ, who is the image of God' (2 Corinthians 4:4).

This is not just a problem for individuals; it infects the whole culture, corrupting, perverting, polluting, imprisoning and deluding to greater or lesser degree the entire structure of our society and its institutions. Our task is to change all that for the better; our lives, our words and our works must challenge the godless status quo. Paul says:

> For though we live in the world, we do not wage war as the world does. The weapons we fight with are not the weapons of the world. On the contrary, they have divine power to demolish strongholds. We demolish arguments and every pretension that sets itself up against the knowledge of God, and we take captive every thought to make it obedient to Christ. (2 Corinthians 10:3–5)

It is not our way to use physical coercion. Nor do we want power. Indeed, history demonstrates with awful clarity that the monstrous fusion of the secular state and the church inevitably leads to corruption. The crown of thorns always sits uncomfortably on the harlot's brow and sooner or later is replaced by a more comfortable and compromising adornment.

Instead, our mission is one of holy subversion. Our role is one of godly influence rather than power, and that influence is exercised through the diffused salt and light witness of its many members. God is at work in the humility of daily service, in the simple ministries of mercy, in the exercise of the greatest power of all – the power of love.

The initial conquest of these islands by the gospel came about not by military might but by people who carried no weapons, who healed the sick and told the simple story of the Saviour in a manner that connected with the culture and innate longings of their hearers. Words, works and wonders is a powerful combination. It is the Jesus way and the apostolic way. It must become our way.

Four proud towers

There is a pragmatic element to this approach also. We face formidable opposition as we seek to evangelise the nation. There are four proud and adamantine towers that stand against us and it is futile to think that we can bring them down by raising up one of our own. Frankly, we will be outgunned, outnumbered and outmatched. Our hopes lie in a subversive approach, for these towers are all built on sand. Eat away at the foundations and they will fall under their own weight. Infiltrate their ranks and they will collapse from within.

Those towers are, in particular and in brief:

The tower of scientism – the perversion of true science

- that denies the existence of a transcendent or interventionist God;
- that believes the whole of reality can be understood in terms of cause and effect;
- that trusts science and technology to solve all our problems;
- that makes the need for a God of miracles redundant;
- that writes off our faith as mere outmoded superstition.

The tower of Darwinism – the evolutionary paradigm

- that obliterates the need for a creator;
- that reduces human beings to the level of animals;
- that spawns both communist and fascist utopian creeds;
- that drives the modern eugenics movement;
- that replaces the return of Christ with the re-creation of man after our own image.

The tower of humanism – the sociological study of human behaviour

- that blames the flaws in human nature on wholly environmental factors;
- that insists we are victims to be treated rather than sinners who need to repent;
- that believes it is legitimate to manipulate our behaviour regardless of truth;
- that says there is then no need for atonement;
- that maintains Christ died for a problem that exists only in the minds of the unenlightened.

The tower of hedonism – the untrammelled indulgence of sensual enjoyment

- that offers guilt-free sex in unlimited varieties, twenty-four-hour sport, shop till you drop, disco till dawn, browse till you drowse, drink till you sink;
- that makes your personal satisfaction the only ultimate value;
- that refuses to give thanks to God for his good gifts;
- that measures life by the abundance of our acquisitions;
- that substitutes materialistic pleasure for true spiritual joy in the Lord.

These towers are tall, strong, proud, well resourced and armed to the teeth. If we try to attack them with brute force we will come off the worse. If we undermine their foundations with prayer, mercy ministry, incarnational Christlikeness, miracles of grace, lives that weave patterns of beauty, genuine love and good works performed by millions of believers on a daily basis, these towers will fall more easily than we imagine!

Respect the journey into faith

So much of our evangelism has relied on the exercise of power rather than the ministry of love. We have shouted, cajoled, usurped, invaded, tortured and killed in our desire to spread the message of the kingdom of love and mercy. Empires have been established with the sword and the cross entwined, and the blood of Christ has mingled with the blood of the conquered. It is not his way.

Winning people and nations is a work of the Holy Spirit. He is the one who comes alongside to help – and that must become our way. Co-operation rather than confrontation. And the time is ripe; many people are searching once again for a spiritual meaning to their lives. It is something we must recognise and it invites us to come alongside people on their journey towards Christ.

It will require us to have a tolerant respect for where people are on their journey. How often have we tried aggressively to present the whole gospel, with the rider that if the person rejects it they might well be knocked down by a bus today and go to a Christless eternity? We insist they choose now. We need to open our ears when someone says, 'But what if I'm not able to choose now? Supposing I have lots of questions? Do you even know me and what I've been through? I'm trying to find answers but it's not that simple. Give me some time, but please don't write me off because I can't take the step you want right now.'

There are many reasons why people can't receive Christ on the spot. Some of these may be vain excuses, but a lot are quite genuine and we need to have love, patience and perception as we seek to help people. It is my own desire that a little of Christ and his message should rub off onto every person I meet. I do not feel obliged to tell the whole gospel at once. Is this fear or ignorance or lack of love on my part? I don't think so.

I am prepared to believe that the Spirit of God works secretly in the hearts of more people than we know.

Rather it is based on my conviction that the Lord wants to reconcile to himself as many as possible and he is patient with us, not wishing for any of us to perish (2 Peter 3:9). So I am prepared to trust that I make a small but significant contribution towards those I meet to help them find Christ somewhere along their life's journey. I am prepared to believe that the Spirit of God works secretly in the hearts of more people than we know. I trust that the unknown passers-by that I pray for as I go jogging in the mornings will one day find salvation. I don't want to pronounce death sentences on people who have not yet committed the crime of refusing for ever the gospel of grace.

Nor is it our job to convert people; that is the work of the Holy Spirit and it is as mysterious as the conception of life itself. We may plant the seed and water it, but God is the author of life – we are not. Sharing the gospel with every man, woman and child on the planet is a whole lot easier than trying to convert them all! Let that be between them and the Lord.

This does not rule out proclamation and persuasion, but those moments come when people are ready for them and if we are not careful we can force people into premature decisions which then go sour. In effect we produce stillborn babies. It requires us to be sensitive to the Holy Spirit and to the human condition.

That said, I believe there is a bigger reason why people cannot always receive our message in one. It is the spiritual despair that lies at the heart of the British psyche.

Ministering to spiritual despair

People from overseas sometimes look askance at us favoured people and wonder why we are so cynical, so depressed and so self-hating. The answers to this are wider than the scope of this book, but there is no doubt that most people in these islands see no hope of having a spiritual life that includes knowing God personally. God is either too great, too mysterious or just too far away. We are practical Deists; we believe that God impassively wound up the universe and then went away on holiday to a far distant galaxy, leaving us to make the best of the machinery. We may pray to him but it is unlikely that our calls will ever get through. Not only are we Deists but we are also Unitarians. God may be the Maker, the Father even, but Jesus was just someone who did better than the rest of us. Indeed, he did so well that he made it to resurrection and heaven. We have no chance compared to him. As for the Holy Spirit, well, we are more aware of ghosts than we are of a good spirit. The best we might manage is a friendly poltergeist or maybe even a saint or two that could help us.

This spiritual despair is confused about suffering and the existence of a God of love. He is either too impotent to deal with evil or too callous, and yet deep down we want to believe in ulti-

If I can't trust bishops, priests, popes, vicars, then how can I trust anyone in the church?

mate goodness rather than ultimate evil. We look at the world and at times we join in with Louis Armstrong and croon, 'What a wonderful world.' Surely there is a wonderful God – but what about all this pain?

If we are confused, we are also disillusioned. Disillusioned with the church. No longer can we hide its disgraceful moments. Historically terrible evils have been done in the name of Jesus by his professing people. Tell me that those were crude and cruel days and everyone was bad, but it won't excuse those who bear the name of the Lamb of God. Tell me those people were not real believers and I will believe you, but how am I to distinguish the difference? If I can't trust bishops, priests, popes, vicars, then how can I trust anyone in the church?

We need a great deal of humility as we approach the world, and the best course of action is to acknowledge without excuse the appalling failings and sins of God's people not only in times past but still today. What we can do is invite people to take a closer look at the New Testament and to see that God takes on people who are not perfected overnight; that the church is not a company of those who have arrived but a community of people who have taken a decisive step in the right direction and who are still in need of much improvement.

We meet many in our society who appear self-righteous. 'I may not be perfect but I'm certainly no worse than my neighbour and I'm no child abuser or rapist,' they will tell you. Yet many a conversation has convinced me that apparent self-righteousness is a front, a defence mechanism against the offer of salvation because deep down they feel too unworthy to receive it.

Some years ago my wife Jan and I visited New Mexico. Much of the country is high desert, arid wilderness, dry rocky outcrops over which the birds of prey hover. It rarely rains and if you wandered across the wastes you would despair of finding water. But there is a river, called the Rio Grande, and there's more than enough water for everyone. If you can find it.

Our nation is a spiritual desert and most people do not expect that we will ever see rain for the soul again. There is no expectation of a satisfying spiritual life, only an endless quest. If the river of life exists then it must be underground or far away; certainly it is beyond the reach of ordinary mortals. Many of those searching wander far and wide. Some of them find temporary and polluted oases, but these often dry up. Some of those oases are called churches, but few settle there. Maybe they pick up what water they can and then move on. A whole lot more try to suck the moisture out of magazine articles, promises of new age fulfilment that they try for a few weeks before sinking back to their spiritless status quo. It's a sad state of affairs and a challenge.

> **It is no use us announcing from billboards that there is a river. . . . We should take the water of life and offer it to all.**

If we want to meet this challenge then it is no use us announcing from billboards that there is a river. The mission mandate, the incarnational call of Christ, is that we should take the water of life and the seed of the word across the desert and offer it to all, seekers and non-seekers alike. People will not come to the water of life unless we can first give them a taste from our own water bottles. We must join them on their journey and learn to share our sustenance with them. Step one in any mission strategy is that we will implement it incarnationally, relationally and patiently.

From Elijah to Elisha

Releasing and empowering God's people requires us to redefine our prophetic nature. Many of us carry a subconscious idea of an Elijah figure when we think of prophets. Elijah was a solitary prophet, a man who appeared from out of nowhere and single-handed took on the entire nation and its government and its heretical religious establishment, calling down fire from heaven and ordering a judicial execution of heretics with a single-mindedness that was frankly scary. Yet this is the image we have of the mighty anointed servant of the Lord: aloof, detached, awesomely anointed, a great preacher calling the nation to repent. If only God would raise up such a prophet, we imagine. That would change things!

When we translate this into releasing the people of God as an incarnational missionary community we can find ourselves encouraging a judgemental and aggressive mentality instead of one that seeks to woo people to Christ. We go forth to war and become a threat to all and sundry. Our witness is individualistic and insensitive; we act as judges calling for repentance rather than healers bringing reconciliation; our words become pronouncements rather than invitations. We want everyone to preach the gospel to all their acquaintances in absolute terms, allowing little room for argument or discussion and taking no account of where folk might be on life's journey. It will produce terrible bigots and a host of embarrassment and wasted opportunities, like the ten-year-old boy who arrogantly told everyone in his class that they were going to hell unless they became Christians and then wondered why he had no friends! We need to be winsome if we would win some.

The prophet Elisha represents a different mentality. Here we have a man of the people who was at home and who much preferred to minister in company. Whereas Elijah came out of the hills, Elisha came from the family farm. Elijah launched a famine; Elisha invited everyone to a barbecue. Elijah was a lone prophet; Elisha was found among the company of the prophets. Elijah needed reminding that 7,000 had not bowed the knee to Baal. Elisha needed no such reminder, for those 7,000 were his friends. Most of Elijah's miracles brought judgement, whereas most of Elisha's brought healing.

We need to serve the world around us with an Elisha mentality. It is the power of love and healing that will impress rather than any amount of divine zapping and declamatory preaching. The fact that we are communal people has far more appeal than our heroic self-sufficiency in God. After all, this is the heart of our faith; we are people reconciled to God and to one another, an eschatological community, a prophetic sign pointing to the healing of the nations.

So, what now?

- The version of events that the world presents is often based on perverse values. Think of situations where you can subvert this from the enlightened perspective of the gospel.

- Grace begins long before we acknowledge Christ. Take your list of people and identify the marks of God's grace in their lives.
- Determine to give someone a taste of the water of life today.

13
Engaging the Spheres

Evangelisation is more than evangelism; mission is more than a crusade. We are seeking no less than the radical and redemptive transformation of society. It can only be attempted as we stand out here in the world. It cannot be done from within the walls of our church culture.

Connecting with the culture

Our problem is one of disconnection. Those who lock themselves in barns soon lose touch with what's going on in the fields. Compartmentalised faith does not communicate, nor do subcultures change history. To be effective in mission we must seize the cultural mainstream and influence it from within rather than try to correct it from outside.

This can come as something of a shock. Many Christians are alienated from the world's culture, and the world is alienated from Christian culture. We are experts at church programmes, but the culture doesn't want our church programmes.

In fact, the willingness of people to attend our churches is determined not by our programmes, be they ever so bright and seeker-friendly, but by the values, felt needs and aspirations of the surrounding culture. A simple question to ask is this: What do people queue up for? Where we live many families get up early on a Sunday morning to visit boot fairs. Something more is taking place than just the search for a bargain among other people's rubbish. Folk queue for the cinema, usually for the more emotionally stirring films and those that address the big questions. Why do they do that in a supposedly amoral and uncaring age? People queue their evening programmes for soaps and soccer. What vicarious longings are being met through these set rituals? People go on training courses to improve their technical, business and management skills. Is it just for money, or do they genuinely want the fulfilment of doing their job better?

Engaging with the culture means connecting with those values, needs and aspirations from within the culture and its structures, rather than attempting to do so from the alien position of current Christian culture. So the arenas for the incarnational missionary community will be those places of shared humanity rather than our rarefied church territory. Whatever the place of Christian schools, businesses, arts centres, political parties and so forth – and they do have a place – what we need are effective Christians in the world spheres, comfortable to be in the culture but ministering the transforming grace of God so that the culture itself undergoes a metamorphosis for the benefit of everyone.

Ancient wisdom

A friend of mine regularly advises top management in industry. He does so as a Christian, bringing the wisdom of the

Scriptures to the boardroom, often to the amazement of managers and executives who never knew these things were in the Bible, let alone their relevance to company decision-making. Needless to say the respect that he has gained provides many opportunities for one-to-one counselling and for sharing the personal implications of the gospel.

Another friend operates a reconciliation service that works right across the board from high level international politics down to teaching children at school how to reconcile their differences. The principles are all there in the Bible.

Others are educationalists applying biblical principles to the very way that we learn, transforming the classroom, whether the subject be mathematics, geography, French or physics. It's another sphere where the Scriptures provide us with powerful tools for transformation.

We could mention the arts and the tentative beginnings of a fresh renaissance that some of us are engaged in exploring outside the church service context. Or what about the reappraisal of government policy on global poverty? Or the application of the gospel to the issues of economic slavery and child labour?

The creation–cross–consummation axis

All of us have a beginning, a middle and an end. So does the history of the world. If we want to engage with the spheres of human discourse and concourse then we must begin where they begin: with creation.

This means identifying with their world, their experience, their feelings, their shared humanity. The first gospel question has to be, 'What do we have in common?' It is a surprising amount once we get over the barrier of our church culture and its weird religious obsessions. I once found myself in the embarrassing position of trying to help a church member through a disciplinary hearing that had arisen because she had abused the vulnerability of a patient in her desire to witness. It became apparent to me that she lacked a doctrine of the normal life. Many Christians live in a pietistic hothouse, nurtured by endless fevered conferences that leave them unable to be normal in the company of ordinary people.

Beginning with creation enables us to connect with people at the level of their reality. Biblical wisdom can filter through our conversation, inform our discussions of everyday affairs and provide some remarkable solutions.

The cross is the place where we engage with the suffering of humanity. It is here that we touch upon the evil in the world, its fallenness, its tragedy and its endless pain. This may mean helping our colleagues though their personal difficulties; it may mean serving the community. Steve Chalke estimates that there are 144,000 Christian mercy ministry projects taking place in Britain. The number is considerably more when you take into account the tens of thousands of community serving projects that never advertise their existence but simply get on with the job.

It is hard to hear about the cross if you never see it enacted in the lives of the proclaimers.

The cross is redemptive. Jesus acted sacrificially to save others. His ministry was for the healing of the nations, and it still is. Sometimes we are called to sacrifice, to lay down our own rights for the sake of others, to demonstrate the gift of restraint, to take the lowly path. It is often the key to releasing intractable situations, and the world will respect us for it.

It is hard to hear about the cross if you never see it enacted in the lives of the proclaimers.

Consummation is where we succeed, and where we say goodbye. Our engagement with the spheres should always be motivated by love and it should have success in mind, be that a job well done, an honourable profit on a deal, students who pass their exams, or winning an Olympic gold. The world will not trust us if we are always trying to come second or third!

Some believers have such a negative view of this world that they live with a poverty spirit that makes everything they do second rate. While the prosperity gospel may rightly be classed as a heresy, the poverty spirit is equally a denial of the gospel. Engaging the spheres means that the hard-working farmer should enjoy the harvest and share that joy with those around.

Life comes to an end: retirement, the end of active service, the closure of a business, bereavement, failing health, the prospect of our own death. The next generation to retire will constitute the biggest people group in the land, a massive sphere in which to engage. Our culture is publicly death-denying, but there is no escaping the reality. While the media exploit the cult of youth, increasing numbers search for answers to their increasing age and declining vitality. We need to bring the rich resource of the Scriptures to their sphere. Many will come to Christ.

Sandy launched a project to help those for whom the end meant premature unemployment and despair. The team helps people back into work. Buddy runs a programme that ensures that every residential care home in town has access to a team that meets the spiritual needs of the elderly. The field is white and ready to harvest! I met a retired man who offered his services as a conductor of funerals. The local undertakers were delighted to have somebody they could call on where the relatives of the deceased had no minister of their own. He told me that he said little in the service but made a point a year later of calling on the bereaved. This act of love found people wide open to the gospel.

Taking the territory

God's people are waking up to the fact that we have lost significant ground over the past decades. Our influence has declined and our message has become marginalised. It is time to take back territory, not in terms of political power – the church always makes a mess of it when it plays politics – but in terms of spiritual, cultural and social influence for good. This is a spiritual warfare and the stakes are high: nothing less than the heart and the mind and the eternal soul destiny of every man, woman and child in the land. The devil won't like us taking back that kind of territory for Jesus.

We need a threefold engagement which involves the airforce, the navy and the army.

The airforce

Modern warfare turns almost entirely on who has the strategic air superiority. Jesus described the devil as 'the prince of the power of the air'. Satan has significant power in the spiritual realm and this affects profoundly the state of the nations over which he exercises this power. This territory, this battle in the heavenly places, has to be won if we are to see anything significant happen on the ground. I believe it is won by prayer, by powerful, mission-focused intercession undertaken by the people of God. The fact that more and more are engaging in this way is one of the signs of hope.

The debate continues about how territorial this battle is, with some claiming that demons only ever manifest themselves through people, and others claiming that they may reside geographically where the conditions are granted for their presence – and equally may be driven out when the spiritual climate is improved by authoritative prayer. I am a both/and thinker on this one, but there are a few points worth making.

It is the equivalent of mounting a campaign about the state of the litter in our street while trying to overcome an invading army.

First, I believe that prayer for territory should be corporate. We've all heard remarkable stories of individuals who have stood in the gap, but this is not the New Testament norm. The man to stand in the gap is the body of Christ, and we need as many members as possible of that body to be mobilised in prayer.

Second, prayer should be addressed to God. Let us not play the fool by reviling the devil or thinking that we control him. The Lord does the rebuking, not us. Our access is to the Father – that is our privilege – and we must not waste time parleying with the enemy.

The third point is to keep in mind the purpose for which we exist: to ensure that every man, woman and child receives the gospel. There are many other agendas that could distract us, but it is the equivalent of mounting a campaign about the state of the litter in our street while trying to overcome an invading army – hardly the greatest priority and, worst of all, fatally distracting.

The navy

The naval engagement is to do with the propaganda war. The wicked are like the tossing sea, churning up muck and mire, and nowhere is this more true than in the realm of ideas. We are exposed as never before to an overwhelming amount of information. Some of this is reliable and edifying; much of it is perverse and destructive. The twentieth century saw the loss of millions of lives across the world through the false ideologies of fascism and communism. We have been indoctrinated with the destructive ideas represented by the four proud towers mentioned earlier: scientism, Darwinism, humanism and hedonism. The nihilism of these ideas has left a vacuum waiting to be filled; people are milling around in a postmodern waiting room, looking for the next train.

That train, the compelling idea that will seize the future, will touch every sphere of life. It is vital then that we address in an apostolic manner each of those spheres, be they business, welfare, government, education, the arts and media or whatever. It is time we pursued an active propaganda war.

That propaganda has less to do with arrogant criticism and bombastic declarations of truth and more to do with asking the right questions and helping not-yet-believers construct a new society in which we can introduce godly values for the benefit of all. What our society needs is not revolution but revelation. We must adopt a creative role if we would win the hearts and not just the arguments.

One of the key areas and a particular interest of mine is that of the arts. I am indebted to Martin Robinson for the origin of the following diagram, which I have slightly modified for our purposes.

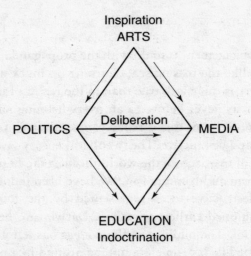

We are all familiar with the game played out between the media and the government. Sometimes it is a serious game; most of the time it is frivolous, but it keeps us reading our newspapers and watching what is called the news but seldom is. I call it by the appropriate acrostic SOAP: Sensations, Opinions And Pictures. It has little to do with the real world, any more than politicians really control the action in a globalised economy.

Yet this game is informed and it does have influence through its deliberations. Traditionally we have thought it was informed by education, so the church has spent enormous resources on trying to influence behaviour and public policy through logic and reason. However, in reality it is the arts that inform the debate. People are changed by inspiration far more than by indoctrination. Whoever can grab the emotions will grab the headlines and eventually the hearts. Government will conform and the rest will be educated into the new status quo accordingly. If the church wants to change the world then it needs to recapture the arts and give a new lead in an age that has become trivial and banal for want of anything better.

The army

The third part of our strategy involves sending in the ground troops. This is where reality bites, for here is the praxis that touches everyday life. Much of this book has been about the importance of mobilising all of God's people into the field, but the harvest field is also a battlefield and we will need to be strategic in how we deploy our human resources.

Experience has shown that the moment a church decides to become an incarnational missionary community it faces a chasm of seeming impossibility between where it is and where the starting line lies. There was an army advertisement a few years ago that presented a gorge with the bridge down and a group of soldiers on one side needing to cross to the other. Viewers were challenged, 'If you are asking "How do I get over?" don't bother ringing us.' Point made. We have to go together and help one another.

The process of transition takes about two years to accomplish using the appropriate materials (see Resources for details). Part of that process involves researching the field, or spying out the land. This is done at every level: the demographical, the cultural, the spiritual and so forth. The research provides the raw data with which to develop specific plans for taking the territory in question.

It becomes immediately apparent that there are key points – strongholds upon which to concentrate our

You may have a supermarket in your field. Why not start a crèche for shoppers and teach the gospel appropriately to children?

attention in prayer, propaganda and praxis. Just as it is unnecessary to kill every person on a battlefield in order to secure a victory, so it is not necessary that we tackle every single issue around us. Research will help us seek God for intelligent guidance. It also shows us the open doors and opportunities. Maybe your patch has a number of commercial and industrial premises. Then why not start a cell group consisting of those who will form a chaplaincy team to serve the staff in those workplaces? You may have a supermarket in your field. Why not start a crèche for shoppers and teach the gospel appropriately to children? Schools invite a whole raft of ways in which to reach every child with the gospel.

In our own church's town we have teams targeting every residential care home and every school, and a chaplaincy to businesses, to name but a few. Looked at like this, the goal of reaching every person in the community is eminently feasible. Add to this the work done by individuals in their streets with initiatives such as neighbourhood houses of prayer, Alpha suppers, Just Looking groups and general good witness to neighbours.

Whatever the specific projects we may engage in corporately, the most important ground troops are us ordinary people acting as chaplains in our homes, our workplaces and our communities, and what we need, of course, is to be inspired, trained and nurtured by a strategically focused leadership team.

So, what now?

- List twelve needs, values and aspirations that are common among the people in your world sphere. How might you engage co-operatively with these to promote the gospel?

- Read the book of Proverbs, marking all those verses that have something to say to the humanity you share with those around you.
- Discuss with your church leaders their strategic plans for prayer, propaganda and practical engagement with the community.

14
Take Me to Your Leader

Identity – our sense of being – is immensely important for our effectiveness at every level of life and particularly so when it comes to our ability to evangelise and transform our nation. For too long we have defined ourselves as God's withdrawn people. We have interpreted the New Testament word for church, *ekklesia* (called out ones), as meaning 'called away ones'. We have hidden our light under a bucket when it was meant to shine like a beacon for all to see. In our desire for purity we have created unhealthy ghettos often characterised by an oddness that we are not even aware of ourselves. Our attempts at evangelisation have been depersonalised and distant, detached from the culture and often plainly antagonistic to it.

Once the paradigm shift takes hold of us and we discover what it is like to begin from the standpoint of the field, the most important factor will be the quality of people we can set to work in that field. Redefining ourselves as an incarnational missionary community, our future will rest with an informal and all-pervasive work-force that persistently bring the grace of Christ to bear upon the world around them, treading God's earth with confidence, challenging the opposition, loving those made in his image and winning them back into fellowship with their Creator and heavenly Father. Key to all of this will be those who call themselves the leaders of God's people.

Leaders matter

I believe in the importance of leadership; indeed, in the terse words of Dwight Smith, 'No leadership, no future.' But not just any leadership. The ability of the church to fulfil its mission in the twenty-first century will depend on the emergence of a very particular type of leader and leadership style. The new leaders will not be stereotypical but they will share a common passion for certain core values and convictions. All of them will have made the paradigm shift.

There is little doubt that we have a crisis in church leadership. Major denominations are struggling to fill their vacancies because few can see the current mode of full-time ministry as an effective way of fulfilling God's purpose for their lives. Many in leadership are wrestling with constant discouragement, while others are doing little more than manage the enterprise and maintain the status quo – somewhat akin to dressing for dinner while the lifeboat is sinking. Many who are growing congregations, too often do so on the basis of superficial soundbites that substitute for visionary policy, quick-fix remedies that replace in-depth strategy, and triumphalist tub-thumping that camouflages lack of real commitment. Meanwhile the tragedy of our unevangelised society continues all around us with its tired, performance-driven workaholics, its gullible, self-destructive pleasure-seekers, its guilt- and pain-ridden victims of broken relationships, its marginalised poor, its directionless children and its media-drugged people without God and without a point to their lives.

It is no time for leaders to be complacent or to bury their heads in the sand, or to protest self-righteously that they are doing their best but they are very busy. Whatever the current state of your particular expression of church, all the statistics for the future are dire. Churches close down at an average rate of one every six weeks in our country. That's 300 a year or 3,000 over ten years. Yet in that same ten-year period no more than about a thousand new churches have been suc-cessfully planted. With most churches at best holding their numbers, unless leadership changes its ways there will be no viable church left in the land in fifteen years' time.

God is speaking clearly about a new paradigm of church, and it requires leaders to change their ways and to do so urgently.

It is no use being soft on church leaders at this time. I know many are stressed, many are wonderful people doing their best, many are sacrificial examples of Christian service, but they are also wilfully responsible for the future of the church. The decisions they make, the style they adopt, the beliefs they stress, the plans they implement, all determine the future. Get that wrong and we all suffer. God is speaking clearly about a new paradigm of church, and it requires leaders to change their ways and to do so urgently. If our churches are to become incarnational missionary communities, they will require a quite different approach to leadership. It is not an option; the old style of leadership will prevent absolutely the emergence of new-paradigm churches and will unwittingly or otherwise play right into the devil's hands. We do not have a decade to consider this matter. By then it will be too late and irreparable damage will have been done.

Nor is this a problem to be addressed simply by the primary leaders of the churches – vicars, pastors and ministers. It is one that must be faced by deacons, PCCs, all those who hold leadership roles, whether lay or full time, whether serving adults, teenagers or children, in whatever denomination or stream you find yourself in. We must change our ways, and fast, for it is equally true to say, 'Wrong kind of leadership, no future.'

I am passionately convinced that we can turn around this dire state of affairs and that we can see a whole series of sustainable harvests, and that social and cultural renewal is possible. We can change the church and we can change the nation. Provided we act. The psychologist Carl Jung observed that when people act it initiates a process that he called synchronicity; things begin to go in our favour. As Shakti Gawain puts it, 'The universe will reward you for taking risks on its behalf.' Or, as we might prefer it, God answers the prayers of those who step out in faith: 'I being in the way, the Lord led me' (Genesis 24:27, AV). Prayers are not answered simply by praying them; we have to take the risks of faith associated with change and set our feet to the path.

Determine to make the paradigm shift

Attempting mere evangelism or missions will prove increasingly to operate on the law of diminishing returns. It really is the day before yesterday thinking if we imagine that the non-relational, non-incarnational, presentational approach of our forebears is going to work any longer. All the presuppositions upon which they could do that, and at times do it effectively, are gone. Our stark choice is simple: enable our church to make the new-paradigm transition, or maintain an ever more irrelevant and slowly shrinking status quo.

I have already indicated that the paradigm shift is a matter of revelation, so it will probably necessitate bringing in a catalyst or prophetic–apostolic ministry to effect that shift. As with any dramatic change of perception, everything will conspire against us. We will find ourselves too busy, moving from one crisis management situation to another; our minds will be filled with questions, doubts and fears. We will consider that we are too old or that this church cannot do it, so maybe we should look for a new posting. Our colleagues will attempt to recruit us for another quick-fix, all-singing, all-dancing package that will consume our energies. We will do everything we can to put off the day. Maybe next year, or when our current five-year plan expires!

It won't do. We have to act now lest we be like those would-be disciples of Jesus who said, 'Lord, I will follow you when . . .' If the penny has dropped with us then we need to ensure that it does so with others. That will require us exposing them to the word of the Lord. We may well find that people in our church membership get the message easier than we did. After all, they live in the real world already. Any opposition is more likely to come from those who have a vested and often heavily biased interest in the church infrastructure itself, and you can already guess who those are likely to be!

Making the paradigm shift is only the first step. There is that chasm of seeming impossibility to be crossed and for that we will need to institute a transition process lasting about eighteen months. (See Resources.) This will involve leadership in thoroughly auditing the church and in doing the primary research necessary to understand the field that God has called us to. It will review every aspect of the church's life and enable the leadership to implement constructive changes that will bring the congregation into a redefinition of its identity and purpose. It will provide the necessary tools for restructuring and initial training of all those involved and will enable this to be effectively communicated.

That takes us to the starting line! From then on there is a fifty-year process to be implemented that will lead to the full evangelisation and transformation of our field and many other fields beyond. During this period we will learn to work with other churches and will see many churches planted as a consequence of our ministry. God being faithful to his word, thousands will come to the Lord and society will undergo a wonderful transformation. Wishful thinking? Maybe. But if the paradigm shift to the mission of God has really got you, if you now understand this new-paradigm church, what else are you going to do with your life?

Yet they will have a new dynamic, for these are no longer gatherings of barn dwellers, but meetings of field workers.

You will not be idle. Your energies will be devoted to envisioning, equipping and empowering all of God's people to serve their personal fields. You will still be holding meetings too. Yet they will have a new dynamic, for these are no longer gatherings of barn dwellers, but meetings of field workers, active missionaries who are together in mission and zealous for the Lord. So expect better meetings.

Training, too, will occupy much of your time. We need training programmes to break the ghetto mentality, to stimulate spiritual growth, to inculcate a concern for the world, to equip the saints to reach the secular person, to research the field, to evangelise effectively and co-operatively, to redefine ministry, to initiate small groups, to plant churches strategically, to produce effective prayer, to make honest appraisals, to work with specialist groups.

Don't attempt this without making the paradigm shift. It just isn't going to work. But once you have made that shift a whole vista of strategic possibilities will open out before you. In the next few pages we will explore some of the pointers but it is not my intention to give you a strategy or a blueprint. We've all too often tried cloning other people's ideas out of context in the forlorn hope that they would work with us. It's time for new-paradigm people to hear God for themselves.

Face your insecurities

If you are an existing leader in an old-paradigm church you may be feeling quite worried. In spite of what I've said, I seem to have done you out of a job. Are you now redundant? It appears that the new-paradigm churches don't really want to meet together on Sundays any more. They don't want religious buildings. They may not even want paid ministry, and even if they do how will we get the money if we don't take up offerings? I seem to have made all your skills redundant too. You are a Bible teacher, a preacher, an administrator of church programmes. Now, it seems, I don't want you to teach in the way that you know. In fact, by the sound of it I don't want you to preach at all – and I want to close all your programmes down into the bargain!

If we don't address these insecurities, you are never going

to make the paradigm shift. Your fear will block your decision-making ability. First, let's recognise that all change is uncomfortable, but without change we cease to be. All of us need the personal renewal stimulated by fresh challenges. Perhaps that's why so many leaders move church after just a few years. Well, you can get that fresh challenge right here where you are from now on. There is enough not only to keep you busy but to keep you stimulated by fresh challenges.

Even so the discomfort may remain. Let me ask you: Did you enter the ministry for a comfortable professional life or because of a call of God to serve the Saviour? There are frankly easier jobs if you want a comfy life. I would get out now if that is what you really want. But if you feel the call of God then you will accept at least a degree of discomfort. As I write this, the thirty-one-year-old colleague of a friend of mine has just been shot dead for the sake of the gospel. My friend, herself a missionary, was upstairs at the time. When many of our brethren serve on the front line, let's not indulge ourselves in too much self-comfort.

Part of that discomfort has to do with learning new skills. We may have been performers; now we are trainers. That doesn't mean we will not perform again. We will still have occasions to preach and proclaim, but we will do it not as the high point of the word of God in the week but as a means of inspiring others to communicate the word where it really counts – on the front line of their lives.

Nor am I saying that we will not meet together. The field workers want to gather to celebrate a week's work and to give praise to God for all he has done through their lives. We will want to party! Nor is our pastoral work finished. Although in the new paradigm we will train a vast number of people to engage in this, we will still have our fair share of cases to handle. In fact, we may well find that we are pastoring many more people who are not yet Christians but for whom we have the requisite skills to assist.

As for all those programmes, well, we will still need good administration, and since many more of our programmes will be in the nature of instruction and training, we will have an ongoing key role to fulfil.

We will also need to train people in many different areas of service, or at least ensure that they are trained. We must cultivate team-building skills ourselves because teams in one form or another are a vital part of the future.

Are you prepared to give it a try? If so, the future beckons.

So, what now?

- Visit your local shopping centre or city centre. Look at the people. This is your field of ministry, and your existing congregation is the means of fulfilling it.
- Write down all your fears, talk about them to trusted advisors and lay them carefully before the Lord.
- Make a decision before God to walk the path of the new paradigm for the sake of Christ's kingdom.

15
Pastures for Pastors

Most church leaders find themselves in the role of hireling, taken on to protect the vested interests of the sheep-fold. Given the prevailing mentality, it is little surprise that many of us become so preoccupied with meetings and programmes and trying to keep everyone happy that we hardly ever get a chance to lift our heads above the parapet to see what is going on outside. Maybe the best we manage is a bit of local chaplaincy work ourselves or maybe a seat on a local school governing body or some such. All that must change.

Loving the land

One of the changes that must take place in our concept of professional leadership is that we should not be taking up a position in a church unless we are specifically called to the field that the church serves. Those with pastoral gifting must see that their call is to shepherd every single person within the catchment area of their church and not just the members of the congregation. Those with more evangelistic or prophetic gifts will want to reach every person with the good news of Jesus Christ and to work for the renewal of the social structures.

Needless to say this cannot be done by even the most gifted or talented soloist – and nor can the task be achieved in a mere five years. In fact, you could not even in the redundant paradigm do justice to a congregation in that time. To serve a field requires a long-term commitment; it demands no less than that we love the land and the people who dwell in it. Some leaders who have understood this are buying their burial plot where they are because they intend to devote their lives to the land and to the community, to see the kingdom of God manifested in a transformed society. Forget the old mid-twentieth-century existentialism; this is not going to happen overnight. Like missionaries of the past, we will have to fall in love with where God has sent us and stay there.

I suggested earlier that the constant moving on of church leaders is one of the biggest contributory factors in the failure of the church to make a lasting impact on its community, let alone to build a true missionary ecumenism between churches. How many times do church leaders really begin to get their act together and engage in some joint venture only to find that one or more moves on, or is moved on by their denomination, throwing the whole enterprise back to square one? We may live in a highly mobile society, especially in our cities, but we need some people who are prepared to become the community leaders simply by virtue of their longevity of tenure and commitment to the well-being of the parish.

I am not saying that leaders should never move on – that is unrealistic – but I don't believe they should do so without having seen their successor into place in a manner that continues and enhances the same vision for the community, rather than leaving their hapless congregation in that hiatus known as the interregnum.

If we truly grasp this we will get to know our field really well and ensure that our people know it. We will prayer walk it. We will be intensely interested in the families, the institutions and the cultural activities. We will connect, and encourage others to connect, to the arts, to business, to politics, to education, to all the institutions of our community, because this is the true sphere of our ministry.

To understand this field will require research at all levels, from the historical through to the demographic and the spiritual. We will regularly be bringing aspects of the field to our people's attention by means of prayer topics, personalities and events. We will encourage every neighbourly activity that seeks to bring the name of Jesus and the people of Jesus into meaningful contact with the members of the

This will not be a matter of sporadic skirmishes but of a committed long-term relational exercise with the people around us.

field. Nothing less will satisfy us than that every man, woman and child in the field knows the gospel really well because we have taken the time, trouble and commitment to ensure that they do. This will not be a matter of sporadic skirmishes but of a committed long-term relational exercise with the people around us.

Field accountability

This brings us to the question of field accountability; that is, our sense of answerable responsibility to ensure that every man, woman and child in a given sphere is repeatedly, incarnationally, responsibly, intelligibly and comprehensively presented with the gospel in all its appealing fullness. Making the paradigm shift so that we stand in the field rather than the barn and determine all our ministry from that perspective invites us to define our field with some precision.

It could be taken for granted when Britain was to all intents and purposes by law Christian, and the church was broken into parishes consisting of people who worked alongside their neighbours, who were subject to the same feudal barons or squires, and who seldom travelled more than twenty-five miles in a lifetime. All that has changed in our highly mobile, diffused and individualistic society where many people are on little more than nodding acquaintance with their neighbours. Even villages have become largely dormitory or weekend retreats for city dwellers, and a sense of community is hard to come by. Add to that the overall decline of Christianity, and the chocolate-box parish church may struggle to make an impact quite as much as the inner-city Gothic pile.

There must, nevertheless, be some form of field accountability, otherwise we will never ensure that the good news reaches every man, woman and child in the land. Mission mandates can only be fulfilled in specific terms, and that comes right down to people by name.

We must also be realistic. Wesley may have said, 'The world is my parish,' but most of us have more modest aims. Few churches can take on a whole town, let alone a whole city, by themselves, especially if this requires a guarantee to deliver the gospel in its fullness to every person. It takes the

Relationships take too long and are too selective. Many people get missed out.

whole church, whether town-wide, city-wide or region-wide, to ensure that the mandate is fulfilled.

So we may define field accountability as when a local church or a group of churches takes responsibility to ensure that every man, woman and child in a given geographic locality receives the gospel in accordance with the church's mission purpose.

Some will protest, for the reasons above, that the field must be relational rather than geographical, and I am tempted to agree. Relationships will play a key role in the process of evangelising the nation. However, the problem with relying solely on relational networks is that we will never get the job done. Relationships take too long and are too selective. Many people get missed out.

Governments recognise this and they see geography as by far the best way of reaching the vast majority of the populace. Hence the geographic wards for election purposes, the local authorities for raising council tax and for providing education and other services in the community. It may not be foolproof but it is far more effective than relying on who the town councillors happen to know!

It makes sense for a local church to choose a field where a substantial number of its members live. This area may or may not contain the church building. Within that selected field there may be institutions and employers that draw people in from other places. That's fine since churches based where those people live will incorporate them into their own fields of accountability. It is also possible to treat these workplaces as joint ventures between mission-purposed churches. Equally, in commuter belts, there is no reason why a number of Christians can't work together in a mobile field called the 0715 from Nether Bulging.

Do relationships have any part to play in this? Absolutely. Everyone knows that the majority of converts come through the relational gateway. It makes sense in a given geographic field to assess and utilise existing relationships as a strategic starting point for evangelisation.

Every individual relationship is potentially a doorway into an entire *oikos* or people group.

Two points must be made: We must look beyond individuals to the people groups or clans that folk belong to. These personal relational smallholdings may be family, social or economic, and they are sometimes described as *oikoi* (Greek for 'households'). Every individual relationship is potentially a doorway into an entire *oikos* or people group. Instead of extracting our one convert from the group, we want to equip that convert to reach the rest of the group. Our model of church will need to facilitate this, whereas at present most churches do the opposite.

People talk of the value of friendship evangelism, but I am not happy with the term. It gives me an ethical problem. Surely it is dishonest to form a friendship primarily in order to convert someone? What do you do once they are saved? Drop them and start another friendship? How many of these can you manage? Real friendship takes time to build and the very nature of such relationships is that they are non-demanding; it is their very spontaneity that makes them precious. Friends draw unspoken lines that determine the parameters of their friendship and if that includes not talking about religion there is little you can do about it. Few of us want the stress of trying to alter our friends, and we don't want them trying to alter us. Nor do most Christians have many non-Christian friends – at least, not after a year in church. We are unlikely to be successful in pursuin[g] where most of our members are inept!

What we do need, however, is friendly evangelism. [B]y [th]is I mean engaging with people in a manner that respects who they are and that takes a genuine personal interest in their whole lives. This is best described as evangelisation rather than evangelism. It is an holistic approach that goes beyond gospel preaching to care about the well-being of the whole person. Friendly evangelisation will begin with existing relationships but it will consciously extend until everyone is reached.

Object or instrument?

The concept of field accountability presents a powerful challenge to existing church leaders. Most, as we indicated earlier, are called to a barn and to serving those who gather in the barn. The paradigm shift requires that in future leaders must show that they are called to the field of accountability and that they see the members of the barn as the instrument for serving that field with the wholeness of the gospel.

Barn-focused leadership sees the gathered congregation as the object of their ministry.

We have already contrasted the barn-focused church with the field-focused. How effectively this is realised depends much upon the attitude of the leaders. If we are constantly harping on about attendance at meetings and volunteers for an infrastructure that we have either invented or felt obliged to sustain then our people will believe that what really matters is the barn – and that realisation disempowers them without anyone even noticing it.

Barn-focused leadership sees the gathered congregation as the object of their ministry. Success is measured by more people, more money, happy people. All you need is an expert in how to run meetings. Well, it's a living but it is not what the kingdom of God is about.

The best we do is create a passive audience that essentially gathers to be entertained in the manner that suits their religious predisposition. However zealously we teach or preach we will always suffer from the law of diminishing returns; people once filled up cannot take any more and since there is no per-

Well, it's a living but it is not what the kingdom of God is about.

ceived outlet for their energies they become gorged on the ministry and some may even begin to vomit. They will express it as 'bored', 'not growing' 'marking time', but it comes to the same thing: they have had too much input that fails to connect with the world of their output. Educated they may be, but most are ignorant when it comes to the dynamic application of the Christian faith to the real world. Pastorally, the most taught may be the most fraught.

What we produce by such an approach is a shamefully limited church. So much potential is wasted or unrealised because there is no dynamic in our paradigm to energise them to live out their faith in the real world. Sure we may urge people to be good witnesses, to be kind to their neighbours, to be honest in their dealings and so forth, but really what we want is for them to come back next week so that we can tell them the same things all over again. We may even talk about everyone being a servant of God but the only real model of what that means is either ourselves or other so-called full-timers.

Once we understand the field paradigm, however, everything changes. The church is now our instrument, our means, of reaching the world. It becomes our work-force, our team. The goals are defined now not in terms of attendance but in terms of going. We want every man, woman and child to receive the good news of Jesus Christ, and the church is going to do it. So our attention turns from mere internal management and programming and away from just imparting information or creating emotionally satisfying experiences. Now we are urgent, impassioned and focused. This field matters to us. What happens in the world around is the crucial measure of the success of our ministry. We are no longer assessed by the quality of our pulpit performance or the number of bums we can put on seats, but by how effectively we can mobilise our people.

So we will want to impart vision and faith. We will return repeatedly to God's great purpose and our instrumentality as his people in the global fulfilment of that purpose. The relationships between our people will matter enormously not simply so that we can keep the peace in public but because these same people will be joint-venturing out in the community and they will be under scrutiny. Our call will be to total discipleship in the everyday, to real sacrificial living, to a glorious sense of fulfilment whether we attended a meeting this week or otherwise. And our people will know it. As a result they will feel affirmed, resourced and empowered to recognise that every gift, every talent, every personality trait,

We are no longer assessed by the quality of our pulpit performance, but by how effectively we can mobilise our people.

each relationship and sphere of activity is a part of serving our Lord Christ.

Spying out the land

Most churches making the paradigm shift will be well advised to begin with a modest field of accountability. The church where I am based has begun with an area consisting of 10,000 people; others have settled for one road. We need to see some achievements within a given time span, and if the field is too big we will simply be overwhelmed.

Whatever the size and shape of the patch – and this needs to be sought prayerfully – we must research the field. This research needs to be demographic, historical and spiritual. Typically, barn-focused churches have only the most general idea of what is around them and it is little wonder that our sporadic evangelistic forays have so little impact.

The purpose of the research is to enable a genuine spiritual strategy to emerge. For example, there is little point in opening an Internet café in the church hall of a residential suburb if all the young people habitually spend their evenings in the high street. Guess where the café needs to be. Nor do you need to establish a specialist ministry to Muslims if you discover that your patch contains just one or two families. But you do need to know how many children live in your field if you are committed to each one being taught the truths of the Christian gospel.

Aside from the demographic information, we will want to assess the spiritual needs. Who are the existing Christians? What genuine gospel communication has already taken place? What alternative belief systems hinder the true knowledge of

God? What ingrained public attitudes cause resistance to the gospel? What known occult activities cloud the spiritual atmosphere?

Research must also project into the future, since the church is engaging in a long-term strategy rather than a quick crusade. For example, are there new housing or business developments in the offing? Have you looked at the local authority strategic plans for your patch?

Research sounds tedious to those who don't enjoy it, but it usually turns out to be quite fascinating and immediately begins to spark all manner of novel ideas for serving the community. From this primary research we can produce some specific and attainable goals over a reasonable period of time. Remember, these are sowing rather than harvesting goals and we should empty our minds of silly questions about how big we want our congregation to be in three years' time. That really is evidence of the old paradigm! The measure of our success lies in the effectiveness of our sowing, not how much we have gathered in our barn. Harvests come in their season.

So, what now?

- Are you in the right place? Walk around your patch prayer-fully until you know the answer. Ask God to give you a vision of what it looks like when all these people have received the good news and social transformation is under-way.
- Begin to sense what the Holy Spirit is saying to the church about its field of accountability. Where is it? How large is it? Does it have satellites?

- The next time you preach, have in mind that this word is for the people outside your building, and the ones inside are going to take it to them. Make this a habit.
- Design an outline plan for researching the field.

16

Shaping Up for Mission

Inspiration goes a long way in a local church. Leaders must impart vision, or if they can't, find someone who can. Yet vision is more than exciting worship, passionate exhortation and appeals for people to come to the front. Vision is literally about seeing. Good leadership means travelling into the future with an imagination inspired by the Spirit of God and seeing what the end result will look like. That's the easy bit! Left at that we have no more than a vision in a vacuum. Leaders have then to return to the present, share the vision and enable their people to take the first step towards its fulfilment. The process will be repeated many times over, and on each occasion people will be helped another step nearer to the desired goal. Leaders who can do this truly have the gift of leadership.

First steps are often the hardest because they involve a basic reorientation of our purpose and direction. Leaders who intend taking mission purpose seriously will need to begin with some kind of statement of intent.

Writing a purpose statement

Mission and purpose statements have been popularised by business in recent years and the church has tended to copy them. Personally, I am not much in favour of producing neat statements that say the obvious without providing any means of testing whether they are being achieved in practice. If the local baker declares, 'Our purpose is to sell bread', I am unimpressed. Similarly if a church says its purpose is to preach the gospel I will nod and say, 'Yes. So what? I never assumed that you made plumbing fittings or grew artichokes!'

However, tell me that your purpose is to communicate the gospel in a culturally relevant and consistent manner to every person within half a mile of your building over the next three years by means of the personal engagement of every member of your church with the community, and I will say that you are taking the challenge seriously. And you have laid the foundations for assessing your progress in a realistic manner.

So if you do produce a working purpose statement, I suggest that it should contain in appropriate words a reference to:

- the abiding mission of God;
- communicating the gospel of reconciliation to every man, woman and child in a given geography;
- the incarnational, repeated and coherent nature of the church's ministry;
- the need for people to face the personal implications of the message in terms of a change of heart and lifestyle;

- incorporation, nurture and equipping in so
  of local church;
- social transformation.

The rest I'll leave up to you!

Redefine your membership

To become an incarnational missionary community requires that we redefine what we mean by church membership. It will no longer be adequate to treat members merely as communicants, nor to view them as attendees at the club meetings. Covenant and club-based approaches to church membership both have the virtue of stressing a sense of belonging to the family of God, and this we must not minimise or deprecate, for if we don't belong how can we expect to function? Yet in many of our churches, for all our talk about belonging, in practice church life boils down to little more than a set of functions.

We expect people to attend and listen to the talks. We want them to show that they believe; that is, they understand the talks. They should conform to our behaviour patterns, meaning we want them to respond to the talks. Those who really progress get to serve in the sanctuary. They set things up for the

In practice church life boils down to little more than a set of functions.

talks. And finally, for the exceptional few, they get to give the talks themselves! A parody? Well, not altogether.

Most leaders have tried to address the problem over recent years by introducing new membership and discipleship courses. Much has been made of home groups to facilitate both spiritual growth and a sense of belonging. However, mostly this has served only to strengthen the extraction model of church – we have succeeded all too well in getting people out of the world and into the institutional life of the church!

The diffused model of church, the *out here/in there* paradigm, sees every member as a recruit for the reconciling purpose of God and called to engage in the battle for truth, justice, love and grace in the world around us. Since every member has a part to play, from the very beginning they need to understand God's purpose for their lives and why God did not take them straight to heaven where they could worship him unceasingly and be perfectly free from the taint of sin. Why did he leave us on earth if not to extend the message of his kingdom into the lives of men and women, boys and girls?

> **We have succeeded all too well in getting people out of the world and into the institutional life of the church!**

The ethos of our initiation courses needs to change from the usual extraction/induction model – which suits joining a club – to a diffusion/equipping model that produces mission representatives.

- Instead of asking how we can get people away from their friends, we should be asking how we can meet their friends. How about a party, or down at the local, or over lunch, or at the school gate?
- Instead of educating people in the protocols of church membership we should be giving them what they need to know to spread the good news among their friends. What about the story of their journey to faith, a basic gospel outline, answers to common questions, praying for friends?

- Instead of asking for their prayers and money we should be asking what support we can offer them in their service for God. Do they need prayer, someone with them, training, opportunities?

Replace all your committees with teams

Treating people as called to serve God doesn't mean producing a lot of unaccountable lone rangers venturing into the field to do their own thing. Jesus sent his disciples out in groups of at least two and this is where we want to put the emphasis: people working together as joint-venturers in the kingdom of God.

Most mission ventures will need to operate in a team context, and the church leader needs to model this in his or her own life. I have been a team player and a team leader for almost as long as I can remember: apart from school football and cricket, where I was disqualified for being endowed with two left feet and a predilection for using a bat as a fly swatter, team has been my life, first in a mischief-making street gang, then in the Boys' Brigade, later on in a large gospel team, and so into church leadership. The pleasure of working with so many wonderful people on many and varied exciting and fruitful projects has convinced me that we should not even contemplate working alone.

Space permits only one or two observations.

Teams have to be put together with a mixture of faith and care – faith that they will work and care that we get the right mix of gifts. It is unwise to put together two people with the same gift spectrum. At best it is superfluous, at worst it will lead to conflict. Nor should we put side by side people of strong but different visions. As the old Chinese proverb has it, 'Two people who talk much will not walk long together.'

We should also recognise that there are Type A leaders and Type B leaders. The first have the shoulders to bear the load and pay the price of change. They are often pioneers and always visionary. The second type are most often pastoral, people-centred and cautious. They seldom do well in a Type-A position but they flourish if they serve alongside a Type A. Two Type As will not walk long together. Two Type Bs will probably mark time indefinitely. But an A and a B can make the foundation for a very successful team.

What people call teams often turn out to be no more than committees. Committees tend to consist of people who are representative of others or who have opinions and influence but very little hands-on involvement. They can be the bane of church life. Teams on the other hand consist of those who have specific spheres of responsibility for which they are accountable. Teams are vision-led and, more often than not, project-focused. Teams are made up of people with gifts and personalities appropriate to the vision and the project. The days of committees should be numbered. People should only be involved in a project if they have a hands-on role to play. Christianity is not a spectator sport at any level.

One of the advantages of the new-paradigm church is the permission that is implicitly given for people to try out novel ideas. Those who pray and plan together are unlikely to degenerate into a mere committee; they are more likely to be thoroughly involved from the beginning.

Shift the control to the edges

Too many of our churches have been structured on centralised control models, often hierarchical in nature and practice. The central leadership determines, vetos or approves everything that goes on. The result is a greatly limited effectiveness, for we can only properly control what we understand, and even the best leaders do not understand everything, in spite of the impression they sometimes give to the contrary!

Centralised control breaks down entirely in new-paradigm churches since the ministry is *out here* rather than *in there* and there is simply no way that a church leadership can control all the action, either in the immediate field of the church or in those personal smallholdings that constitute the fields of influence exercised by their church members.

Nor should they. What can I control when a group of colleagues start a cell group in their office canteen, or three members join the local kite-flying club to bring the kingdom of God to bear on its members, or when a businessman sets up a Christ-centred counselling service for fellow business leaders? What do I know about hospital management that qualifies me to exercise control over three of my church members who want to commence a prayer network within the hospital? Is my authorisation really needed when one of our reps meets with fellow reps for a weekly cell group in the diner at Membury Service Station? What must I approve when an executive in a global company meets in a cell with others from different nations in whatever country they happen to be in at the time

We need enabling leadership that consciously shifts the power to the ever-expanding edge.

and who consider themselves to be a computer-networked expression of church that even shares a virtual communion service together?

We need enabling leadership that consciously shifts the power to the ever-expanding edge where the lives of the church members interface with the lives of non-Christians. This kind of leadership positively encourages entrepreneurial activity, especially outside the church programme. Such a leadership feels the need not to manage but simply to impart vision and skills as appropriate, and to provide pastoral support. The result of such leadership is a massive release of church resources in a multitude of previously unconsidered areas.

In the church we attend it has led to an innovative ministry into residential care homes, a brilliant ministry to teenagers, enabling them to say no to sex before marriage with dignity, a re-employment centre for the long-term unemployed, a business chaplaincy project, a community project that touches a thousand people a week, and much else besides. The leadership makes no attempt at all to manage these projects or the people concerned. All that is provided is vision, skills and nurture, and all of this is itself delegated so that no one person or central team carries the whole load. This is to say nothing of those initiatives taken by twos and threes that never make the church headlines. It means that the influence of the church extends far beyond its plant or meetings.

Centralised control models have their roots in the secular world. Jesus said, 'You know that the rulers of the Gentiles lord it over them, and their high officials exercise authority over them. Not so with you. Instead, whoever wants to become great among you must be your servant' (Matthew 20:25–26).

This radical stance obviously refers to our heart attitude as leaders towards others, but I believe it goes further and challenges the very structures we employ. There is little good in having a servant heart if we operate in a master-controller structure. We need to change our structural models.

Many years ago I came to see that the old pyramidal model was faulty. You know the one: at the top is the pastor/ vicar/priest, followed by the deacons/elders/churchwardens, followed by the departmental heads/home-group leaders, followed by the male members of the church, followed by women and children, followed by dogs, cats and gerbils. I have seen this model defended as biblical because Jethro advised Moses to delegate the less important judicial decisions to others. Tendentious exegesis to say the least! Jethro was advocating delegation but there is no suggestion that he was expecting Moses to be top of a hierarchy, and even if that were to be argued, we are surely speaking about the dispensation of the law rather than that of grace. In the New Testament we look in vain for hierarchical structures of leadership. That isn't to say that those with a pre-existing paradigm in their heads can't find texts to support their case!

If centralised control models are pyramidal, then decentralised enabling models are matrix-shaped. Instead of a chain of command, there is a total interconnectivity between the members of the team, allowing the power to operate at the interactive edges rather than from the authoritative centre. The only task of the leader is to maintain vision and engender sweet relationships. This is an organic paradigm, a body model, and it is the way that neurones and synapses function in the brain, allowing a remarkable unity of overall function without the dominance of any one part. Increasingly, it is a model used in secular business, leaving church leaderships in the old paradigm not only severely limited by their structures but looking increasingly out of touch and amateurish.

This will sound very threatening to control freaks – and many leaders are. We fear the ensuing chaos, the lack of accountability, the irresponsible actions that might arise. Well, I have seen leaders cause just as much trouble while operating in their centralist roles. There is no perfect, safe system and, in spite of having encountered any number of claimed biblical models, I have seen that all of them are subject to failure because of the human element. We have to take risks; it's just a matter of determining what kind of risk, and personally I would rather trust the Spirit of God at work in the people than trust in one or even a few power hungry paternalistic leaders who claimed a virtual monopoly on the wisdom and anointing of God.

So, what now?

- Together with others produce a draft mission statement and invite people to pray about it.
- Revise your induction and discipleship courses in the light of God's mission purpose for your church members.
- Do a thorough review of all the committees and teams in your church. What adjustments need to be made?
- Pyramid or matrix? Which model are you currently operating under?

17
Power to the People

All sorts of people fulfil leadership roles in our churches and organisations, but leaders are not the be all and end all of the ministry. Indeed, their very expertise may actually disqualify them from ministering to the people in our communities. People don't relate well to experts. They do relate to church members who have the love, grace, humility and relationship to serve their neighbours. Recent research has demonstrated that when people are in trouble their first port of call is the family and their second is a well-trusted friend. The experts and the professionals are far down the line. Furthermore, the average Christian is much more in touch with the realities of life than the minister, who spends most of his mornings in the study, the afternoon either visiting church members or attending committees and the evening in conducting church meetings.

Words, works and wonders

Every-member ministry, chaplaincy in the market-place of life, means empowering, training and nurturing a whole congregation in words, works and wonders. If you have any kind of leadership role in the church, whether minister, elder, deacon, youth pastor, children's worker or home group leader, you need to play your part in this.

Words

Our people mostly encounter friends and colleagues who have no gospel framework in their lives, no language for spiritual talk. Our job as communicators is to provide the language for our people to make the crossover without the need for translation or interpretation before they can do so. It is unfair to leave that work to our hearers. It means an extra step in our preparation, asking ourselves to what extent people without the background can understand our message. My rule of thumb to preachers is to imagine that their entire congregation consists of pagans and to preach accordingly. It is a very healthy exercise!

Works

The call to manage such a spiritual work-force requires leaders also to ensure that their lives are full of good works. This means that we must not demand so much of people's leisure time in attending meetings that they have no time left to serve others. It means too that we must train them in how to do their daily jobs as good works performed in the name of the Master. This training will include workshops to develop interpersonal skills, conflict resolution, biblical ethics, transformational prayer, work–leisure balance, good neighbour skills, family life – in short, skills for living an out-here life. Needless to say church leaders don't have to do all the training!

Wonders

When will we truly believe that the Spirit of God rests upon his people? Leaders do not have the monopoly on miracles, though to hear some of them you would think so. We need to train and encourage our people in responsible prayer for the sick, for the provision of miraculous supply for others and not just for themselves, for divine interventions. 'May I pray for you?' can be a powerful act of love, especially impacting when the prayer is answered. Of course, there is a risk element in all this. Let God's people loose and you never know what might happen, and most of us have at least one nutter in our churches to justify our worst fears. However, it is a risk that can be minimised by proper discipleship and accountability, and by ensuring as far as possible that people do not work solo.

DRIP feed discipleship

Earlier I wrote about the spirituality spiral, the need to equip our people with certain attributes that would make them effective chaplains in their homes, workplaces and communities. How we do this, the methodology we use, is crucial and I want to suggest a learning model that I have dubbed DRIP feed discipleship. No, I don't mean take a few drips and feed them! I mean using the natural learning process.

This process is familiar to most parents because it's the way children learn language and other basic life-skills. It is also known as no-way-back learning because once acquired it cannot, apart from serious trauma, be lost. Whenever I plunge into the sea or a swimming pool I never doubt that I can swim. When I get on a bike I don't question whether I can ride it.

These are instinctive skills because I learned them in such a way that I cannot unlearn them.

Much of our discipleship teaching has been done differently. We have imparted information that we believe people need to acquire, based upon logical and systematic doctrine. We have hoped that somehow, after our ten-week crash course, they would put it all into practice in their lives. That seldom happens and we are then faced with the difficult task of repeating information about what they should believe for the rest of their days. Our mistake is to think that there is a block in understanding, that we have not explained it properly or that they are dull of hearing, or even wilful in heart. The real fault, however, lies in the assumption behind our methodology. It is the assumption that people are changed by education.

In reality people are changed by inspiration. A child learns to speak because he or she hears others speaking and is inspired to do the same, but a child cannot be taught to speak by receiving a crash course in English language and literature. We have to begin with the felt need of the child, with the current level of experience, and build on that. Which brings us to how DRIP feed discipleship works. DRIP is a simple acrostic:

Describe
Reflect
Instruct
Pray

It forms the basis for a long-term discipleship process that all of us can participate in and works best on an individual or small group basis. It is ideal for cells and similar groups.

Describe

Beginning with real-life experience we describe a current situation. It may be a workplace scenario where someone is trying to form a better relationship with their difficult boss. It might be an issue within the family, like why I get so ratty with my husband.

Reflect

Having described the scene, we reflect on the situation under the guidance of a mentor. This allows us to ask questions about our responses and reactions, where we thought we or the other person went wrong and what effect the situation has on others and on our own wider life and spiritual growth.

Instruct

Given this information the mentor then imparts, or better invites, exploration of appropriate teaching. This may be from the Bible, it might be of the 'what would Jesus do?' variety, it might be accumulated Christian wisdom. Either way, it is teaching applied to this particular situation.

Pray

This is followed by prayer, and the encouragement to put the teaching into practice.

What happens next week? We follow it through, we re-describe the scene, reflect on the changes, instruct some more, and pray into it again. In this way our disciple slowly and naturally undergoes a process of transformation through the renewal of their mind, and lessons learned this way are never forgotten; they become instinctive.

We have used DRIP for a number years now with considerable success and the methodology is implicit in much of Jesus' training of his disciples as well as Paul's epistles. To the objection that it is too subjective, we answer that true theological understanding is always born out of life experience rather than the academy, and that at least those taught this way are putting into practice what they learn.

DRIP feed discipleship challenges us as leaders to consider whether we want to impress people by our performance or whether we want them to be impressed by their own. Are we the stars or are they? The old models of learning saw the people as empty buckets to be filled from our abundant spouts. Today we think in terms of cybernetic loops. Doctrine is woven into the life experience of student and tutor alike, and life experience is woven into doctrine – what I believe shapes who I am and who I am shapes my beliefs and the Spirit of God overshadows the whole process.

What about preaching and teaching?

Much of our preaching and teaching as church leaders has been based on the assumption that our people have a basic framework of ideas into which they can fit the content of our message. These ideas include a belief in God and redemption, the notion of a Messiah, law and grace, and so forth. While this may be a valid assumption for cradle-to-grave church-goers it can by no means be taken for granted among the population at large. Most people do not have such a framework today.

It means that we must tailor our approach according to the audience that our congregation interacts with in their daily lives. The book of Acts gives us four useful models.

1. Acts 2. Peter's Pentecost sermon makes massive assumptions. He can assume that his Jewish audience understand their theocratic heritage, that they know the Law and the Prophets, that they expect a Messiah. Such preaching is appropriate when presenting the gospel to those reared in a Judaeo-Christian church. Traditionally youth camps have proved fruitful reaping grounds for the seed long and patiently sown into the lives of those from Christian homes who have attended Sunday school all their lives.

2. Acts 10. When Peter addresses the Roman God-fearer Cornelius and his household the Holy Spirit falls dramatically on the hearers before he can finish his message. Cornelius represents the decent, honourable person who respects Christian values and is characterised by moral rectitude. Peter talks about Christ. Because Cornelius respects God there is no need to bring him under a conviction of sin. Instead, the Holy Spirit meets Cornelius's real need: a mighty disturbance to his middle-class, self-controlled respectability. Before you know it these respectable people are speaking in tongues and prophesying like Pentecostals! It's Toronto Blessing for toffs! There are plenty out here who need that today.

3. Acts 17. Paul's sermon on Mars Hill in Athens addresses people lacking a Judaeo-Christian framework. They know nothing of the Old Testament or the Jewish roots of the faith, they have no messianic expectation, they don't even believe in

one God! Paul starts where they are, noting their interest in religion, their superstitious belief in lucky charm gods to help them through the vagaries of life. Instead of condemning this he acknowledges their shrewdness in including an altar to the unknown god. From this jumping-off point he describes God as the Creator and sustainer of all things, uncontainable, transcendent – yet we are set in our world, in our own time and place, so that we might seek God in the hope of finding him. He is closer than we think, for in him we live and move and have our being. A new age of enlightenment is dawning and it's time to change our thinking: justice is coming. A man will put things right and to prove it God has raised him from the dead! This approach is the most relevant to the majority of people in our contemporary society.

4. Acts 19. Paul addresses disciples of John the Baptist – people who honour a great guru, ascetics who want self-improvement. They have undergone a religious ritual that expresses their repentance from the moral licence all around them, but they need to encounter Jesus and to experience the Holy Spirit. Paul's approach honours his hearers' desire for a better lifestyle but it adds the dramatic new element of an encounter with Christ. Many new age types, and some in the sects, can find a response to an invitation to experience the fullness of Christ when presented thus.

Abstract theology produces distracted listeners.

Preaching to an incarnational missionary community requires us to model how to communicate with their world. Like Jesus, we will make much use of parable and metaphor. We will dispel the charge of being boring not simply by improving our technique but by ensuring that we connect with the reality of the human condition, both inward and outward. Abstract theology produces distracted listeners.

Real-life preaching means addressing honestly and regularly the three big questions that lie behind the soaps, the lunch-time conversations, the news headlines, the dramas and the serious songs of our world:

- Why do the innocent suffer?
- What is happening to moral standards?
- Why does religion cause so many conflicts?

The lecture is not necessarily the best way to do this. Many people learn best by hearing stories, by soap operas, by narrative tales into which truth is interwoven. Others learn best by interaction, by hands-on engagement with the theme. They do not like to sit still for long, but will happily participate in a journey of discovery. There are others who learn best from the big visionary picture, who appreciate multimedia presentations that fire the imagination and inspire outrageous possibilities of faith. Still others prefer an orderly presentation of facts and a compartmentalised structured approach to learning. Our task is to address all four types of learning pattern. It is unlikely that one preacher possesses all the skills needed to do this, and this is an area where team ministry comes into its own.

We should also address the Jesus questions. Whatever real or perceived problems people have with church, they seldom feel badly about Jesus. True, not everyone believes that he is the Son of God, but most acknowledge that he was a good man, a great moral teacher, a miracle worker even. Generally he is viewed as a man who dared to suggest that love was a greater virtue than power and that he paid the ultimate price for that principle. Many are now happy with the idea that he might have risen from the dead.

Jesus is cool. So let's talk about him. I describe myself as a dedicated fan of Jesus. That means I'm a real follower of his path, a disciple if you like. As with all fans, I consider myself privileged and enhanced to be one, and I am enthusiastic about him. I can tell you all sorts of things about him too. I know more or less what he looked like: strong, muscular, outdoor type, used to handling tools and conducting his business, Middle Eastern Jewish features (olive skin, brown eyes, dark hair, bearded), normal height. I can tell you that he loved being with people, and was always good to have at a party. He enjoyed his food and his wine and beer. I know about his mother and his adoptive father, and his brothers and sisters. I know where he was born, where he grew up, the kind of education he received, the church he attended, the languages he spoke, the environment that helped shape his life and so forth.

Whatever real or perceived problems people have with church, they seldom feel badly about Jesus.

I can tell you with even greater certainty about many of the words he spoke, the miracles he performed and the hope he brought. Jesus was so far ahead of his time that we have nowhere near yet caught up with him. Then there is his death in all its untimely pathos and profundity. What happened when he died and God raised him from the dead? It is awe-inspiring, amazing, but incontrovertible. Jesus is alive, and he's in the place of highest honour spiritually. If you press me further, I will tell you that I discovered this to be true for myself, and when I pray I know that by his Holy Spirit I have a personal relationship with him that is simply amazing.

So I have three questions to ask and to invite exploration. They are these: Are you a follower of Jesus? Do you have a problem with Jesus? So why aren't you a follower of Jesus? Simple and to the point.

Equipping our people to serve God includes teaching them the simple enthusiasm of fans who find it easy to talk about their favourite subject and, in the nicest possible way, are always on the look out for new recruits to his fan club, otherwise known as the church!

So, what now?

- What do you give most attention to: your performance in church or the performance of your people in the world? Begin to adjust your values and priorities.
- Set up some experimental DRIP feed groups.
- Prepare your next sermon on the assumption that not a single believer is present in the congregation. Make this a habit.

18
Workers Together

We've all sung the song 'Seek ye first the kingdom of God'. We pray, 'Your kingdom come.' But what do we mean? Possibly we simply hope to have a lot of converts and a full church building on a Sunday. Perhaps we have in mind the numerical and spiritual success of our own work, and that sometimes at the expense of others. We want our denomination or stream to come out on top. At least, that is how most church leaders in practice function. Yet any educated understanding of the kingdom of God tells us that the kingdom is far larger than the church and certainly larger than any denomination. In fact, since the kingdom of God is the totality of creation visible and invisible, when we pray for the kingdom to come we pray for the values of that kingdom, the will of God from his throne, to be manifested in every facet and sphere of human existence. The church may be a vital instrument of the kingdom, but to limit the kingdom to what goes on in our church is patently foolish.

Affirm your people

We must face the wider challenge. No longer can we limit our responsibility simply to putting on church programmes or managing the plant known as the church building, or to visiting the needy and fulfilling speaking engagements. From now on our major task is to equip the saints for their work of ministry, which is twenty-four hours a day wherever they are.

> It may be that we will run fewer church programmes, but we will make much more church progress.

To do this we must constantly cast vision so that our people understand fully that they are all full time for Jesus and that their lives count all of the time. The ground is holy wherever they stand, not just in the church sanctuary. We must concentrate our attention on the need that our people have to feel affirmed and empowered to live for Christ without feeling that we somehow disapprove of them going to work, spending time with non-Christian friends or enjoying a day out. It may be that we will run fewer church programmes, but we will make much more church progress. We will have more times of fellowship and perhaps do fewer organised activities. We will pray for people working in their secular environments and not simply for those who are full time.

One of our very simple practices is to get an ordinary person out the front on a Sunday and interview them about their daily employment, and then invite prayer and words of encouragement for them. It sends out an unmistakable kingdom message: we believe that you and what you do matters to the mission of God.

We will also seek to encourage skills acquisition. This does not mean us doing all the teaching. Some of us have a particular gift for explaining the Scriptures and making them relevant to real life, but many of the required skills for that life are best taught by others who have the professional expertise. Let's not be afraid of using non-Christians appropriately – we might even influence them towards Christ!

One of the problems of traditional leadership roles is that the leader is expected to be a multi-talented, all-singing, all-dancing expert on every facet of life, when God has placed within the body of Christ a multitude of skills that can be passed on for the benefit of others. Even in the relatively simple social frameworks of the early church milieu the older women were charged with the responsibility of training younger women in household management. How much more could we do today, utilising the skills of people who have learned how to do well at their sphere of life and at the same time to express the kingdom of God in their daily activities? Why ask a church leader when you have people around who can do this from experience?

Many of these skills relate to what we said about every-member chaplaincy in the home, the workplace and the community. Some concern the activities that we put on as corporate projects. It is great to have enthusiastic volunteers, but what about their training? We too easily mistake zeal for skill. Leaders of mission churches will ensure an ongoing training package for everyone who is involved in their church projects.

Our other responsibility is to provide appropriate support structures for our people. Again these need to be delegated and we should develop pastoral support teams rather than simply leaving it to the pastor or elder.

Many of us in the new paradigm are evolving pastoral care structures that begin with our commitment to care for every person in our field of accountability, limited only by the extent to which we have earned the permission to care. Obviously most of that care takes place among those who are committed to the church or who are at least on the fringes, but the model is deliberately designed to focus on the mission and to make it impossible for the pastor to go it alone! So, for example, we might use a home or cell group to provide day-to-day pastoral support and to exercise some form of care ministry to the not-yet-believers around them. We may develop a skilled team to handle the more difficult and personal problems that people present, akin to a general practitioner's role in medicine, and reserve the senior leaders as the equivalent of hospital consultants for the really tricky cases – and they in turn may refer on to specialists as required. Mission is not evangelism at the expense of care; it is care extended evangelically into the whole community by the whole Christian community.

Mission is not evangelism at the expense of care; it is care extended evangelically into the whole community.

Local leadership, local church

A vital part of kingdom thinking is to divest ourselves of the notion that every local church must go it alone in order to preserve and propagate their angle on the truth. Strategic field accountability, as I have already intimated, requires us to recognise that whatever God is doing he wishes to do through all of his people. There is only one body of Christ and it consists of all true believers identified in a plethora of local congregations that subscribe to the historic apostolic faith. Irrespective of our differing traditions we are called to fulfil this mission mandate together. It will mean that our individual fields of accountability will overlap. Provided we agree that the existing members of other churches are off limits, this need present no problem; there are plenty of uncaught fish in the sea and the church leader too incompetent to go catch his own, resorting instead to stealing from the local fishmonger's, is frankly pathetic!

Church leaders need to change their attitudes towards one another. We may no longer dare to claim superiority over others because of the apostolic tradition of our denomination or its doctrinal purity or the trendiness of our services. I am well aware of all the issues involved in this process of finding one another, but the bottom line at local level comes down to love, trust and humility – virtues that Christian leaders should excel at!

One of the most encouraging signs in the land is the phenomenon of local church leadership prayer meetings that are springing up everywhere. Indeed, a town, city or region where this is not taking place can now be said to be out of order and its church leaders in need of urgent repentance. Personally, I will not attempt to minister mission strategy where church leaders have not begun to pray together for their shared population. Leaders who do pray regularly for the field, release a blessing from heaven and produce a conducive climate for the gospel seed to flourish. They also create a spiritual strength and unity that provides moral leadership for the surrounding culture.

The future will see much more joint-venturing as those church leaders who are learning to pray together for the good of their shared communities begin to trust one another and to realise that they have much more in common than that which historically has divided them. In one town where I work this has reached the stage where a number of formerly independent church leaders have informally covenanted together, with an openness for other leaders to partake, to unite in long-term mission for the gospel of Christ in their town. They have declared that they will

- be one in spirit and purpose;
- in humility honour one another in their various callings, above themselves;
- look out for each other's burdens and interests as if their own;
- do nothing out of selfish ambition or a spirit of competition;
- continue to meet together to work out the details of this partnership.

It serves as a good example of what it means to seek first God's kingdom, and doubtless he will bless it.

Get zoegetic

Working together with our people and with other leaders is more than a matter of organisation and activity. The quality of our shared spiritual life is all-important and that comes down to the intimacy of our own relationship with God, our prayer life, our allowing the Scriptures to speak to our own hearts, and our dependency upon the Spirit of life to energise all that we do and are. Jesus is the way, the truth and the life.

We may be good at directing people, we may be experts at teaching truth, but can we impart life?

This hit me with blinding force one day, and the impact was shocking. I realised that most of the people I ministered to were mules, self-sterile offspring of a stud hired to increase the stock in the stable barn. Very few were fertile and capable of producing spiritual offspring themselves. Then I looked around and saw that this was the condition of most churches. Studs were hired and when they were spent a new one was brought in, but the majority of the people, the converts, were not able or willing to reproduce their faith – and some of them really were as stubborn as mules!

What had gone wrong? What was missing? By now I had seen that the paradigm was all wrong. What did we expect, given that we were working in a framework that made us the most spiritual and most important people in the church? Why should it even matter, provided we kept the numbers up by dint of our spiritual fertility? Yet the moment we change the paradigm and embrace the mission of God, it becomes crucial. If the ministry is all of God's people all of the time, then those people will need to be as spiritually fertile as we ourselves.

It led me to coin the word 'zoegesis', derived from the Greek words for life and for genesis. I define zoegesis as the ability and the desire to reproduce offspring who themselves will be zoegetic; that is, they will also possess both the ability and the desire to reproduce in their turn. We need both; in the natural world a couple may be fertile but lack any interest in having children, or even any interest in sex. Equally, someone may have all the desire in the world but be infertile. Ability and desire must go together if you want babies.

There is no doubt that many good church leaders have both

characteristics and produce a number of spiritual offspring. Some of these are themselves fertile, but how do we address the issue of such low fertility in most of our churches? I suggest that it involves vision and training, but more importantly the work of the Holy Spirit. When Hannah cried, 'Give me children or I die!' she was asking for more than a child. What she wanted was a family, a clan, a tribe, a nation. She wanted to be known as an ancestor by her descendants. I believe we leaders must cry to God with the same passion and vision, and we must extend that desire to embrace all those in our congregations who are known to be spiritually fertile.

Life, real spiritual life, like all life comes from God himself. He is the vital source, and all the research done in genetics has failed to explain the mystery of life in merely mechanistic terms. Even should that be possible, it will not adequately explain human consciousness and the spirit of human beings. So too with spiritual life. We may develop the most excellent packages for church growth and development. We may understand the culture of our market-place, know how to communicate intelligently and persuasively, but that will not produce the mystery of life. For that we must seek God himself.

> **The real measure of our spirituality . . . lies in our ability to bring the presence of God into people.**

The real measure of our spirituality does not lie in our ability to bring people into the presence of God; it lies in our ability to bring the presence of God into people. Where he is, there you will find life. If this is to happen, we shall have to seek God ourselves and develop a whole new openness to the Holy Spirit. This is not the world of the spiritual public performer. Conception, life impartation, takes place in secret and nobody is fooled. Either you have it or you don't. The proof will be in the production of a baby.

Yet zoegesis asks a further question: Is the offspring also willing and able to reproduce? There is not much fooling here either. Those who have it will soon demonstrate the fact by the impact they have on the lives of others, by the good works that bring glory to God's name, by the impartation of Christ to others, by people coming to Jesus and finding salvation through their instrumentality.

I have found this profoundly challenging. Unless I keep being refreshed by the life-giving Holy Spirit, I shall produce nothing. If I don't keep my life pure – that is, free from conscious sin and idolatry and self-seeking – then genetic faults will enter and my offspring will be unable to reproduce. At best, I will be used up; at worst I will fail totally.

At a time when we desperately need a spiritual renewal, when so many have been lost from our ranks through the privations and casualties of a war against the faith that has seriously weakened our numbers, we need more than a few super-studs in the pulpit. We need a fertile membership that will produce many spiritual children and as soon as possible. This is a matter for earnest prayer, not only on our part but on the part of all those who have life. And who knows whether God might not do some miracles of grace and grant fertility among the sterile? Leaders, get zoegetic!

So, what now?

- Look at all your church programmes in the light of whether or not they prioritise empowerment, training and care for our incarnational missionary community.

- Do you meet regularly to pray in the kingdom of God with other church leaders in your vicinity who are not of your denomination or stream? If not, why not start?
- Begin to pray for fertile children in the light of a vision for a society transformed by God's life-giving grace.

19
Unlimited Possibilities

Having read thus far we may feel daunted by the task, especially if we are church leaders. It all seems so huge and challenging. That is understandable and perhaps not entirely our fault. Most of what is taught in our theological and Bible training colleges is firmly rooted in supplying leaders for yesterday's paradigm. Even those that talk about mission usually do no more than produce 'mission and . . .' courses. Few leaders have made the paradigm shift, and there are still relatively few churches in the land that have. So the challenge is to pioneer, as well as to reach the nation with the gospel, but perhaps the least that can be said is that this one purpose will keep us from adding anything else to our agendas! There's enough here for a satisfying lifetime of ministry.

Probability and possibility

People sometimes question us about the probability of reaching every man, woman and child in our nation, let alone of transforming our culture. Is it not unrealistic? Are we not batting above our league? Hasn't it all been tried before?

There are several points to make in reply. First, this is not a call to convert every person in the land. That is a matter between the individual and God. We have done more harm than good when we try to collect scalps from heads that are not yet ready to roll! Our task is simply to ensure that the message is properly communicated.

Second, it is eminently feasible. If we mobilised only half our existing church members so that each one reached one other person with the gospel in the space of a year, and that person in turn did the same, it would take us no more than seven years to have completely re-evangelised the nation. This is an achievable goal.

Third, there is a difference between probability and possibility. Probably, we won't do it; possibly, we can. Dwight Smith, to whom I owe the great debt of having clarified my thinking on this whole subject, speaks of the difference between probability and possibility thinkers. Probability thinkers probably won't; possibility thinkers possibly will. Leaders must be possibility thinkers. Indeed, real leaders are possibility thinkers; they are by definition people of vision. 'Can do', rather than 'can't do'; seeking solutions rather than bemoaning problems.

I am inspired by the astonishing achievement of those who set out to banish the scourge of smallpox from the planet. The vaccine had been available for decades but by the end of the Second World War the disease was still rampant. The World Health Organisation took the decision to abolish the disease; it was possibility thinking. The only way the scourge could be vanquished was by vaccinating every vulnerable person on earth. On a small budget and from a small office in Geneva, these possibility thinkers set about their task. They did so in a world still riven by war and with many parts difficult to access.

Two strategic decisions turned their possibility into reality. First, they trained a vast number of ordinary people who were capable of administering the vaccine and of training others to do the same. Second, they went to where the people lived. The implementation of these two principles has, apart from the current dread of military use, rid the world of the terrible disease.

We may not be able to vaccinate people against sin, but the least we can do is put the vaccine and the instructions on how to use it into the hands of all who need it right where they are, and we can do so by mobilising our people.

Redemptive gateways

Who is reachable and saveable? Old-paradigm church restricts our vision of what God wants to do. It has too few gates and they are often too narrow. Apart from children's and youth work it is only really possible to come through the main door of the church service or, if you are a non-career female, via a women's meeting of some kind. And when we do engage with the needy in our society there is often a considerable gap between the mercy ministry to the outcasts of society and the main body of the church. Few make the full journey.

Jerusalem and the temple had many gates and they ranged from the Beautiful to the Dung. These two alone might act as a metaphor for reaching the world. Some undoubtedly will come through the gate of arts and culture; some will come through the gate opened for the refuse of life. Others may enter via the Old Gate because of their age or culture. There are those who will come via the East Gate from different ethnic traditions. Maybe evangelists bring their converts through the Fish Gate and perhaps pastoral carers bring theirs through the Sheep Gate, while charismatic types may enter through the Fountain Gate and the burned out via the Water Gate. I don't want to overwork the metaphor but simply make the point that being a missionary community means recognising and creating a number of quite diverse redemptive gateways through which people can come to Christ.

Out-here church begins where the world is and recognises the differing needs and situations found in the population. We know that one size does not fit all. Some congregations are better geared than others to meeting particular needs; some aspects of a community suit the seeker better than others and the only way to find out is to engage with people where they are.

The research that we do in our field of accountability, and the personal knowledge of our acquaintances that we can collate, will tell us much about what turns people on. It is our task to open appropriate gates for them. The point of a gate is that it allows easy access rather than having to climb over the wall. Boys' Brigade was the gate for me because it offered a chance to get out of home for several nights a week and indulge in gymnastics, table tennis, snooker and sport in general. Sunday morning Bible class seemed a small price to pay. You would never have got me into Sunday school, let alone through the medium of the church service. A good redemptive

Ask yourself how many parties you host for the benefit of the sinners. Jesus would feel more at home in such a church!

gateway serves the would-be entrant, not the gatekeeper.
Gateways are born out of the culture around us, not out of the
church culture.

A key gateway today is the party. Almost any kind of party.
People in our society love to party, whether it is the classic
booze and dance, or the evening around the pool table during
a sales conference, or the lingerie party, or the get together
with friends for a few drinks, or . . . whatever. This is how we
form our relationships and increasingly how we conduct our
business. The party may be a get together down the pub, it
might be a dinner party, or a picnic, or a rave. People party;
so let the church party! Food and drink and a chance to meet
people is a major secret of the success of Alpha. Ask yourself
not how many services you put on for the benefit of the saints
but how many parties you host for the benefit of the sinners.
Jesus would feel more at home in such a church!

Belonging before believing

There is an irreconcilable tension involved in being in the
world but not of the world. As a result the church often
lurches from one extreme to the other. Sometimes it is lax and
the quality of Christian life inside the church is no better than
the carnal lifestyles of those outside. Other times see the
church reacting against 'worldliness' until there is almost no
connection between Christians and non-Christians.

Our desire for purity can make the journey very difficult for
genuine seekers. We keep them at a psychological and sometimes physical distance unless they make a full profession of
faith and pass through all our membership hoops. It means
that much of our evangelism is predicated by the assumption

that non-Christians are lost, corrupt and liable to poison a church if they are brought any further than the contact necessary to present them with the gospel.

The believe-before-you-can-really-belong approach allows only a narrow fringe of searchers to come within our compass and it does so treating them as having no value unless they can say the magic words 'I've asked the Lord into my heart', or some equivalent terminology. A lot of this thinking arose out of the existentialist approach to conversion evidenced in the Billy Graham crusades of the 1950s and 60s – everything was Damascus Road stuff with no place for the journey.

In this postmodern world, such an approach will cut no ice; people want genuine relationships, they want to be treated as whole human beings and to be appreciated for their own sakes, not simply for their pattern of beliefs. If we want to see people come to Christ, they must be genuinely welcomed into our midst and they must feel that they can make a true contribution to the life of a community without compromising either their own current position on the journey to faith or the fundamental beliefs of committed Christians. We must accept social and communal belonging before belief and not the other way round, whatever the technical grounds our tradition requires for formal church membership.

In one of our church plants we had a family where the father had given his life to the Lord but the mother had steadfastly refused. Over several years, as folk treated her with real respect and love, she became more and more at home with us and ceased to be hostile. The breakthrough came when the pastor of the church began some leadership training for key people, including the father of this family. The pastor invited the unbelieving wife along as well. As a result she began often to turn up on Sunday mornings with her husband and daughters. There came a day when she gave her life to the Lord. No one was compromised by this – neither she nor the church. Nor did she ever fool either us or herself that she was a follower of Jesus until she really was. Today, following her baptism, she is a zealous believer along with her family.

The believe-before-you-belong approach nurtures a cultural paranoia that always fears to be tainted by too close a contact with non-believers. Such paranoia acts as a serious barrier to people coming to Christ, and makes it really difficult for us to involve them at even the most superficial levels without them picking up the scent of our disapproval. For paranoia doesn't come across as fear; it conveys instead arrogance, superciliousness, pride, disdain and contempt.

Reaching our world means that we need the doctrine of the normal life that allows us to engage freely with our culture and its people, keeping ourselves from obvious sins but treating people as our equals if not our betters, honouring their talents and their contribution. Churches doing this make more impact than those that don't, because they get nearer to the heart of Jesus.

Once we form relationships with not-yet-believers and

The one condition is that we are first prepared to receive people as fully functioning human beings.

demonstrate that we appreciate them as human beings with a contribution to make, there is no reason why we can't begin a quiet discipleship process. In fact, by example it will already be taking place as our people work alongside them. They will pick up our way of looking at life with Jesus. Recently, having a new roof put on our house, we ran into a technical problem that necessitated calling in the building inspector. The likely solution would have been costly and disruptive, and the inspector in question was known to be a stickler. I prayed, and when the inspector came we found a simple and effective solution to the problem that was amazingly easy to implement. Naturally the builders were delighted, but they got to know that I considered it an answer to prayer! It taught them that prayer is a valid way of living. I did not need to give them a series of Bible studies on roofing!

Many people are willing to follow the open-plan approach of Alpha courses with its opportunity to learn about the Christian faith without needing to be fully committed first. The one condition is that we are first prepared to receive people as fully functioning human beings. Such an approach theologically puts a far greater emphasis on common grace than some church traditions are prepared to tolerate, but to neglect common grace is to do despite to the divine order and to neglect the universal applicability of the covenants of creation and post-diluvian providence.

I am not advocating compromise or moral and spiritual laxity, but we need to remember that the wrong kind of purism has more in common with the Pharisees than it does with Jesus. He at least understood what Roman Catholic author and priest Andrew Greeley was getting at when he wrote, 'God draws straight, but he uses crooked lines.'

Funnels or trumpets?

I have come across instances where church leaders and mission specialists have talked about the funnel model of Christian discipleship. It works like this. You do some general outreach to a lot of people, maybe children in Sunday school or in some youth programme. A few of them show interest, so they begin to enter the funnel. Some profess faith and they, this smaller number, go deeper into the funnel. A smaller number still become committed to church membership and get really deep in, and a tiny number become excellent servants of Jesus Christ and these are the ones who get right through the funnel.

We should reverse the model and turn the funnel into a trumpet.

I believe this model to be quite false and destructive to the work of the gospel. It reflects an extraction mind-set based on a paradigm that assumes only very few will be saved. It is pragmatic for a dying church but totally inappropriate for a mission church.

I suggest instead that we should reverse the model and turn the funnel into a trumpet. In other words we take whatever number of people we have, be they Sunday school children, young people or non-Christian friends, and ask ourselves from the very beginning how we can equip them to fulfil God's purpose in their lives, irrespective of whether they have made a profession of faith. Instead of filtering them out in the old elitist system, let's democratise the gospel truly and offer all that we can to all that we have and measure our success not by whom we have left at the end of the process but by the degree to which we have imparted grace into the lives of all of them.

Since the Christian life is a journey rather than a number of hoops that we are meant to jump through, let's not worry too much whether people make all the right noises at the right times. We will be surprised by how many more converts we have and by the number of people who will hold us in high regard for the input we had into the success of their lives, even if that doesn't always accord with our more rigid parameters of faith.

Such an approach, of course, assumes a genuine love and commitment to individuals, but that is surely precisely what the gospel is about. Training people as though they were children of God even before they have professed faith is a faith statement, an affirmation of possibility, in itself. I would sooner have ten people I could nurture so that they multiplied their potential to reach others and fulfil a divine destiny, than have a hundred from whom I might extract ten. And my ten in the trumpet model will reach far more than ten from the extraction model, for the simple reason that the extraction ten are already damaged by the implicit elitism of the paradigm. At best they may add a few, but they will never multiply.

The prophet Isaiah said to the barren people of God, 'Enlarge the place of your tent, stretch your tent curtains wide, do not hold back; lengthen your cords, strengthen your stakes. For you will spread out to the right and to the left; your descendants will dispossess nations and settle in their desolate cities' (Isaiah 54:2–3). The possibilities are as limitless as the grace of God.

So, what now?

- Write down the possibilities that could be fulfilled if your church were wholly mobilised into the field. Dream some dreams, wish some wishes, lay them before God and ask for faith.
- List the gates that are open for people to access the gospel.

How many qualifying marks do they need before they can enter?

- Find a few people whom you can help fulfil their life potential in Christ.

Glimpsing the Future

As individuals and churches make the paradigm shift, as we evolve into incarnational missionary communities that set out to evangelise the nation and to work for social transformation, what might we reasonably expect? God's word always accomplishes his intent and if we sow the seed and water it with prayer it is reasonable to expect a harvest – indeed, a big one. Perhaps better still we will reach a situation where we start producing a series of sustainable harvests. Yet these harvests will not have come through the route of big evangelistic campaigns; there will be little head counting and data processing. The growth will be organic and diffuse. Weed fields will slowly become wheat fields, the dry desert will blossom like the rose, and we will hardly have noticed it any more than we watch crops growing. It happens quietly and steadily.

Planting for growth

No longer will we be content to store seed in the barn of our self-interest; instead we will plant it back into the field so that it can multiply. It will change the shape of church to come and lead to many more expressions of church to meet the needs of twenty-first-century people. These churches will be shaped by the culture of the people rather than that imposed by ecclesiastical diktat. We will see, for example, the emergence of football club churches, dance churches, jazz and folk churches, kite-flying club churches, factory churches, supermarket churches.

Michael Moynagh, projecting some possibilities for the year 2020, suggests that the church will express itself best in a multitude of dissimilar models as it seeks to communicate the radical demands of the gospel in a culture that requires that church must fit the consumer. Some of these churches will be in halls of residence, some in football clubs, some in support groups; most will not meet on a Sunday, lots will be in workplaces. Most will find ways of expressing their unity with the rest of the body of Christ through electronic audio-visual links. Denominations may evolve to be some sort of seal of quality, but most church plants will be undertaken as a result of local co-operation between churches and not out of denominational exclusivity and competitiveness.

Some of these experiments are already taking place, and they are likely to emerge as a major factor in church growth and expression over the next decade. There are many obvious issues to address, but one thing is certain: we should not expect new converts necessarily to join our existing expressions of church. Frankly, they are too alien, and no amount of seeker-friendliness is going to overcome that for the vast majority of previously unchurched people.

This may sound fine, but who wants to plant churches any longer? The hard facts are that the recent interest in church planting, encouraged with the best of motives by movements like Challenge 2000 in the 1990s, has proved a mixed blessing. Not that church planting is anything new, of course. When the gospel first reached this nation from Ireland, the missionaries naturally planted churches wherever the good news took root. The Roman and later Anglican expressions of church ensured that every part of the land had a parish church. Following the Reformation and the rise of nonconformity, many churches were planted outside the established parish system, notably by Methodists, Baptists and later Brethren and Pentecostals. The twentieth-century proliferation of denominations saw wide-scale church planting to reflect the doctrinal and cultural distinctives of those denominations.

In the latter part of the century there came the conviction that church planting was an effective means of church growth, and therefore a strategic way of evangelising the nation. It was, however, flawed thinking for several reasons.

- First and foremost, locked into old paradigms we produced mostly more of the same – churches that were conceptual clones of the original model and only marginally adapted to their new situation. Although often highly evangelistic in their early years, the majority were barn-focused models trying to attract new customers into their shop rather than infiltrating the community. Highly energetic modernising movements in the process drew substantial numbers from existing churches, causing much resentment and heartache among leaders who were unconvinced, unwilling or unable to compete. Church planting becomes threatening as a consequence.

- Many new churches relied on the commencement of a meeting and the erection of a building in the style and expression of their particular denomination, but with scant reference to the cultural needs of the target community. Local Ecumenical Projects have suffered from the difficulty of bringing together people of different traditions and seeking to accommodate everyone's preference in the forms of liturgical expression, while the world around found all the forms irrelevant.
- Others tried church planting by splitting an existing congregation into two, often on the basis of geography and in ways that rode roughshod over people's established relationships. As a result churches carried a considerable amount of bereavement in their spirits and, although recovery does take place, few are anxious to repeat the experience in a hurry. Many of us have made that mistake to our cost.
- The existing models are further complicated by the mixed motives of the founding members. This is seen at its most acute when a group of dissatisfied individualists, frustrated for want of more freedom, go out to start a new work. Most of these self-destruct within five years.

Some church plants , however, do succeed very well, and many a new housing estate and regenerated inner-city development now has a vibrant church. A good number of the so-called house churches of the 1970s have now matured into well-established works, and many of their corporate-style initiatives nowadays do produce genuine converts of their own rather than relying on the wandering sheep of other churches.

For all that, the idea of rapid evangelistic church growth by means of church planting has failed to capture the imagination. As we noted earlier, recent research from the major church planters in the denominations and streams indicates that no more than 1,000 new churches were planted throughout the decade of the 1990s and this takes no account of the number of churches that closed during that same period.

So should we abandon church planting as a means of church growth and simply concentrate on growing our existing congregations as large as we can? I want to suggest the opposite: rather than give up on church planting we need to plant tens of thousands more.

Multiplication church planting

There are several reasons for large-scale church planting, and the first is the simple observation that our existing church buildings are insufficient to contain any significant growth in numbers. Even the modest post-Second World War numbers would not fit in.

Second, the demographics of the nation are changing rapidly and many a town no longer has sufficient expressions of church in the right places. The town where I live, for example, has a cluster of traditional and new churches meeting in its centre but virtually nothing at all on the new estates that have sprung up around the perimeter. It is a familiar picture. True, many more people are mobile, but church is meant to rely not on the motor car but on the ability of God's people to infiltrate their community with gospel living. This is an even more crucial factor in our densely populated cities where unless a micro-community has a viable expression of church within its boundaries it will remain a ghetto of unbelief.

My third reason has to do with cultural permissions. Unlike the United States and many emergent nations, most of our conurbations have arisen by the joining up of villages. Indigenous British people are historically village folk and prefer a small number of intimate relationships to amorphous masses. We like to belong; we like people to know our names and to recognise us in the street. We are the nation of pubs and clubs, and our soaps and dramas constantly reflect this fact. Even young people living in cities, while having little to do with their neighbours, nevertheless like to find a bar or bistro where they can hang out – 'third places' are environments where we can be intimate without being isolated.

Many of our culturally imported models of church planting failed to recognise this reality and rooted in the unconsciousness of the average church leader has been one simple paradigm: growth – we must grow a large congregation. In terms of real growth this can never work. Our culture will not permit a congregation to exceed more than about a thousand members and that only in rare circumstances. It is no model for the nation.

Coupled with this misconception is the underlying belief that the chief manifestation of church is the Sunday congregational meeting, an idea as unbiblical as it is unreal to modern life patterns.

I wish to propose instead that we begin with the needs of the field and that church planting is seen as the most effective outcome and instrument of serving those needs rather than our particular denominational emphasis or personal preferences for meetings. I suggest further that this needs to be encapsulated in our vision for mission from the very beginning so that every person understands and anticipates such an outcome.

This especially applies to leaders of small groups, be they called cell groups, home groups or whatever. Leaders of these groups need to be taught not only to produce new groups but to look for the clustering of such groups into local church expressions.

The proper consequence of this approach is that we will abandon mere addition models and establish multiplication models. This is easier said than done, because the addition model is deep in our thinking and it takes a change of perspective to think multiplication. One of our leaders some months ago asked the congregation the simple question, 'What is the fruit of an apple tree?' The good-natured people answered, 'Apples.' His wife then piped up, 'More apple trees!' That's the difference between an addition and a multiplication ministry. What would you be most instinctively happy with? It reveals whether you are living in an old addition framework or whether you have grasped the concept of taking a nation for Christ.

This came home to me recently when I told a successful church leader in a seaside town that I could see what the town would look like with a thousand new churches. He thought I was mad – which I probably am – but I realised that I was coming from a multiplication model and he was coming from an addition model.

What I had in mind was a thousand churches of around fifty to a hundred members. In other words, something culturally indigenous and birthed from the multiplication and clustering of small groups, rather than a dozen more preaching centres that would touch relatively few of the population. How will these churches manifest themselves? That isn't the prime consideration, because they will all be different, shaped by mission, not pre-formed for mission. Missiology must precede ecclesiology.

Multiplication, or saturation as some would have it, church planting is not the first step. It can only take place when the church has regained its purpose, its health, its local unity and its fertility. However, as these factors become realities, we should expect to be multiplying churches to the point where corner-shop Christianity is the norm and where the most influential group of people in your street are the ones who consider themselves members of the MyRoad Church.

Some will wish to challenge my thesis by suggesting that British people do like large gatherings. They go to football matches, rock concerts, raves and race meetings. This is true, but they do so normally in company with their regular group of friends and relatives, and they do so because it is some sort of celebration. Yet even here it is worth noticing that cinemas have long gone multiplex to account for people's preference for a more contained setting, and supermarkets are rapidly recognising that many people prefer a smaller expression of the brand rather than travelling out to the shopping mall.

The idea of many diverse but relatively small congregations does not militate against large gatherings for celebration. It's just that my idea of large is 100,000, not 5,000, and for that to be a reality it can't be every Sunday unless we are prepared to sacrifice some of the very things that will help us reach that happy state. To make congregation into celebration is to lose intimacy and local impact.

It is easier for churches that are essentially local already to grasp this concept, but much harder for churches that draw from a wider area. The larger of these latter have often invested a large amount of money and personnel into their public showcases and these vested interests are resistant to change. Living truly for the kingdom of God will require sacrifice from these churches, both in planting out into barren areas and in making their facilities available to groups that are not of their particular denominational persuasion.

We have already seen this at work when an ethnic church is birthed in an area and an English church makes its facilities available for their use. Why not do the same for a group of English people? Our willingness or otherwise will reveal whether we really have a heart for the kingdom of God or simply for our own petty empire.

Use your imagination. Stroll around the streets in your patch. Think of every road with several home groups. Imagine those groups under good leadership defining themselves congregationally as belonging together to serve their community. Imagine them committed to multiplying themselves wherever a number of home groups has come into being. Imagine your local stadium filled with such church expressions and the local leaders in unity encouraging more and more such plants. It's enough to keep you busy for a while, but it is not a mere pipe dream. If we believe that the heart of God is for every person in our communities and that the gospel is God's power, then it is eminently possible.

No limits

We live at a time when globally we are seeing the greatest expansion of the gospel that there has ever been. Much of it is occurring in countries that we traditionally thought were the places where we sent missionaries. Now those countries send missionaries to us. It demonstrates that God is faithful and that the seed sown really does produce a harvest in its season.

It also shows that the barriers of expectation fall where God's people understand outside-in living. Numbers that we in the Western church only dream of become a reality when ordinary people are released by the extraordinary power of the Holy Spirit to set about the transformation of their nations. It can happen here. We can transform our nation if we want to, and there are no limits to what the Lord might do through our lives.

There is no need for us to jet off to a holy mountain far away, or to give up our families and homes and livelihoods. All it takes is for us to change how we think and to put into practice the implications of that change. It's challenging; it's exciting; it's possible – in our lifetime the earth really can 'be filled with the knowledge of the glory of the Lord as the waters cover the sea' (Habakkuk 2:14). You may be a leader or just an ordinary fan of Jesus, but let me end by asking you this question: Are you willing to take the risk of faith that will usher in a great harvest and prepare the way for the return of the King in clouds and great glory? If you are, there will be no limits to your future fruitfulness and fulfilment in Christ. You really will begin to transform the world.

So, what now?

- Dream some ridiculous dreams. How many incarnational missionary communities could you envisage in your area?
- How are you training your key leaders for multiplication church planting?
- Decide whether you will put this book back on the shelf, or whether you will act on it.

- If you are not a leader, why not talk to a leader about the part you can play in the mission of God?
- Walk around your neighbourhood. Write down the homes where you would like to see home groups established. Where would you like to see congregations set up? Lay this before God. Go back to it once a year and see what has transpired.

Resources

John Houghton is available to advise church leaders on making the paradigm shift to incarnational missionary communities. He can be contacted at Catalyst Ministries, PO Box 303, Hailsham, East Sussex BN27 3XS or at johnhoughton@gioserve.co.uk

Catalyst Ministries publishes the two workbooks used by John:
Mission Now – Motivating for Mission
Mission Now – Making the Transition

Together in Mission publishes the workbook *Journey into Mission Church*, along with supporting videos. It also sponsors 'Leaders for a Mission Church', a three-year distance learning MA course in new-paradigm church leadership.